Sidonia's Thread

Sidonia's Thread

The Secrets of a Mother and Daughter
Sewing a New Life in America

Hanna Perlstein Marcus

Cover design and graphics by Kay Green, Green Graphic Design

The epigraphs used at chapter openings are taken from *Coats and Clark's Sewing Book: Newest Methods from A to Z*. Educational Bureau, Coats and Clark, New York, 1967. © Coats & Clark, Inc. Reproduced with permission of Coats & Clark, Inc.

Unless otherwise credited, all the illustrations that appear in the book are the author's.

In the addendum, the first illustration, the Dachau concentration camp questionnaire for Laura Perlstein, prisoner number 86795, is from the United States Holocaust Memorial Museum, International Tracing Service (ITS) collection, document number 10237950. The second illustration in the addendum, the death certificate for Dezso Perlstein, prisoner number 57569, from Dem Sonderstandesamt Vorgelegt, is an ITS–created certificate dated March 3, 1952, United States Holocaust Memorial Museum, ITS collection, document number 45817270.

The characters in this memoir are based on real people but have been given fictitious names. In some cases the author has used the characters' real names, with their permission.

ISBN–13: 978-1466345034

ISBN–10: 1466345039

LCCN: 2011918021
CreateSpace
North Charleston, South Carolina, United States of America

To my mother, Sidonia Perlstein, who gave me unconditional love and taught me to stand up straight

We dance round in a ring and suppose,
But the Secret sits in the middle and knows.

— Robert Frost, "The Secret Sits"

Contents

Prologue

My mother died on Mother's Day, that second Sunday in May when we Americans celebrate motherhood by paying homage to the women who sacrifice so much for the sake of their children.

For all my childhood, it was just the two of us. Yet my mother had gone to her rest on that Sunday morning without ever revealing my father's identity or the truth of my conception. It took me a long time to figure things out, struggling to piece together clues through her old correspondence and photographs. I never told her about my discoveries, worried that I might drive her to the point of madness. At the end, we both had our secrets, each confident that the other knew nothing of her darkest, deepest mysteries.

My mother was a very deliberate woman. Everything she did had a method, a reason, a purpose. She had a grand plan for me, her daughter, her only child and closest living relative. But she never divulged it to me as I developed into the perfect, yet often reluctant, model for her fashion acumen and imagination. Our relationship revolved around her ideas for creative design and her ability to implement them by pushing thread through a needle with her hands or through a sewing machine. My job was to wear and exhibit the handmade clothing, eliciting the inevitable admiring looks and comments that came from anyone who had the pleasure of viewing them. Her job was to achieve fulfillment through the praise of all those who saw her creations, and to make sure I did not slouch on the job.

We came to America from a displaced persons camp in Germany when I was two years old. It was in 1949, and we rented a room from a widow who lived in the north end of Springfield, Massachusetts. It was there that I started to collaborate with my mother to display her masterful stitchery, yet there was a dark secret that hovered over our bond for all the years of our life together.

I had no father growing up. Yet I sensed at a very early age that the subject of my father, who he was and the reasons for his absence, was forbidden in our household. So I kept my questions about my paternity bottled up inside for more than fifty years, vowing never to hurt my mother by bringing up the events of her life in a displaced persons camp. Then, on the eve of her move to elderly housing, I discovered the cache of letters and photographs that finally gave me clues to my real identity. Combined with a visit to my mother's home village in Hungary and a lone interview with her recorded on video, I uncovered the secrets that changed my view of her forever.

Throughout her sewing career, my mother owned only one sewing book, *Coats and Clark's Sewing Book: Newest Methods from A to Z*, a gift in 1967 from an appreciative recipient of her design talents. Although I never learned to sew myself, I instinctively knew that if I were ever to recount the story of our life together, I would accomplish it metaphorically through the chapters of this sewing tutorial. Therefore, each chapter of this book is titled by a sewing technique and related quotation from the 1967 first edition of *Coats and Clark's Sewing Book* that suits the events portrayed in that segment of the story.

No metaphor is more important than *thread*, incorporated into the book's title. "Thread" represents Sidonia's vision for her daughter's future and her weaving of stories that tie early twentieth century Hungary to twenty-first century America. It creates the texture of a family that her daughter never had as a child, her great artistic gifts as a designer and fabricator of beautiful garments, and her chosen method of bonding with the child she loved.

When the few remaining souls who knew my mother before she came to America, except one, refused to grant interviews about her early days, I abandoned my original idea of including intense genealogical research and dialogues with friends and relatives. I decided, instead, to write a deeply intimate story based primarily on memory and my mother's personal documents, with only a few genealogical references, preferring to stretch my imagination and test my fantasies.

My mother passed away in 2006, aware I was writing about her life. She would have been satisfied and proud of my memories about our journey together to make successful lives in America and gratified by my veneration of her supreme talent as a fashion designer, creator, and maven. Yet, she also would have been terribly wounded by my revelations about the secrets she had tried so hard to keep from me for so long.

As I wrestle with the guilt of divulging such painful truths, I often talk to my mother as though she were still alive and tell her that it is better this way. Finally, the burden of humiliation and disgrace has been lifted, and the world can come to know my real mother, whose strength of character and courage were so significant that, as opposed to denouncing her in shame, the angels call to one another in praise of her honor.

Acknowledgments

Writing a memoir about Sidonia and me was an emotional undertaking, one that I was not sure I could accomplish. For a while, I tried to sort through the events of our life together, the documents I had uncovered, and my feelings about all of it on my own. Yet, after a year of failed attempts at writing a coherent story, I knew that I would need others to help me dig deeper into my psyche to pull out my true feelings about the extraordinary bond between me and my mother.

The story began to take shape in 2007 when I met Lisa Oram, a developmental editor, who artfully drew out my memories of the relationship between Sidonia and me. Chapter by chapter over a two-year period, she helped me to understand my true emotions about events that occurred in my childhood and continued into adulthood. During our collaboration, I finally crafted a story that portrayed great love, resilience, exceptional, wonderful talent, suffocating secrets, and sheer determination and perseverance. I owe Lisa a significant debt of gratitude for laying the story's foundation.

I am a product of my long-term service in local government, and my closest group of friends come from my time with the City of Hartford and the Town of Manchester, Connecticut. Although I have little family, I am fortunate to have steadfast, devoted friends, most of whom have supported me in all my endeavors over many years. A select group of them took the time to read my manuscript at various stages of completion and offered their invaluable advice and feedback, much of which has been incorporated into the final version of this memoir. My heartfelt thanks go to Eleanor Beaulieu, Diane DeFronzo, Sue Heller, Beth Stafford, Deborah Stein, Diane Wicks, and Paula Zeiner, not only for reading the manuscript, but also for their continuous loyalty and encouragement.

I owe special gratitude to a recent friend and second mother, Tillie Sheptoff, one of the best readers in the world, who read my manuscript, offered her insights and perspective, and (if I may be so bold), has become one of my first "fans."

One person in my circle of friends is also my copy editor, Nancy Simonds, who has acted as a mentor and adviser in moving my story forward and in helping me decide my next steps. Nancy's knowledge led me to my final editor, Lorraine Alexson, a foremost literary craftsperson, who provided form, style, and shape to the manuscript, giving it its finishing touches before publication.

My appreciation also goes to Ira Fink, who understood the value of marketing and promotion early on and succeeded in placing photographs and articles about my story in the local press.

I am especially grateful to Simon Fuchs, my lifelong friend and significant other, who has read the manuscript starting with its earliest version. His candid and thoughtful comments, ongoing guidance, and frequent patience helped me to determine the proper publication path for this book.

To my grandchildren's *bonne maman*, Lucile Urvater, who has always shown great interest in my story and has her own story to tell, I owe many thanks for reading the manuscript and for thinking enough of it to talk about it with other authors and literary connoisseurs.

Many thanks go also to Elizabeth Sandy, my mother's friend from Germany, who shared some of her memories of the Bergen Belsen displaced persons camp and Wentorf with me. When few others would talk of that time, she opened her heart and recollections to me, offering key kernels of information to better understand my mother. When the occasional Hungarian word required translation, she was also swift to supply it. I look forward to hearing more of her memories.

Rabbi David Edelman, the principal of the Lubavitcher Yeshiva, where I attended as a child and is still its dean, whose incomparable devotion to his faith and his students are recounted in my memoir, read the manuscript in one sitting. He called me immediately, obviously beaming with pride that one of his students had written a remarkable and heartfelt story about her early days in Springfield and her vivid remembrances of the yeshiva. His observations and encouragement mean more to me than he can possibly know.

I thank my children, Brenda Marcus Bula, and Stephen Marcus, the funniest, smartest, and most talented people, each in his or her own way, whom I have ever known. They have given much to this book. I sometimes think that these children knew their grandmother even better than I did. Their special knowledge of her, and of me, allowed them to provide me with the kind of advice only they could share. They are truly the family of which my mother and I always dreamed.

I owe a special debt of gratitude to the staff at the Survivors Registry and Holocaust Survivors and Victims Resource Center at the United States Holocaust Memorial Museum for their noble and painstaking work in sorting through millions of pages of documents to find those relating to the Perlstein family.

As well I thank the Coats and Clark Company, which gave its permission to reprint portions of its book, *Coats and Clark's Sewing Book: Newest Methods from A to Z*. I had always hoped to develop my story as though I were embarking on a sewing project to create a garment, using a step-by-step approach to the task. As a nonsewer, my mission seemed daunting and sometimes virtually unattainable. The Coats and Clark book and the company's kind cooperation have made achieving my objective possible.

Look, Hani, von of my customers give me a sewing book. It's my first von.

Do you think it will help you to sew better, ma? I joked, picking up the large orange book featuring a rose-pink spool of thread, a sewing needle, and a four-holed button on the front cover, and two pattern pieces and a tracing wheel on the back.

No, but I like et here in my sewing room. It show I am a serious sewer, she responded, as though not aware that the world already knew.

I glanced at the book's title, *Coats and Clark's Sewing Book: Newest Methods from A to Z*, destined to be the only sewing book she would ever own, and laid it back on her table.

1 Pressing

The practice of pressing a stitched seam before it is crossed by another, and all details as they are finished — is perhaps *the* Golden Rule of Good Dressmaking. . . . In pressing . . . use a light, sliding motion without ever letting the full weight of the iron rest on the fabric (this might leave an impression, or, if done on right side, cause a shine). — "Pressing," page 157

1952. She had a way with thread. When she sewed by hand, her right middle finger, shielded by a steel, dimpled thimble, skillfully pushed a threaded needle through the fabric. While sewing, she possessed the concentration of a sculptor molding clay into the desired shape, unfazed by the world around her. The thread produced neat, precise, fine-looking stitches of even lengths — in finishing a hand-worked buttonhole, sewing a hem, tacking a facing, or basting sleeves — and represented her best means of communication, speaking more eloquently than any verbal language.

At the sewing machine, she could loop a spool of thread through the machine's levers, knobs, tension points, needle, and bobbin with her eyes closed. Her right foot applied a measured, steady pressure to the foot pedal, causing the fabric to flow smoothly above the needle plate, as though propelled by a continuous gust of wind.

It was most likely my mother's way with thread that attracted people like Mrs. Alpert to her. Mrs. Alpert gave us our first home in America. We shared a room in her two-family, turn-of-the-century house at 44 Brookline Avenue since shortly after Independence

Day in 1949. Located in the north end of Springfield, Brookline Avenue prided itself on maintaining its Victorian persona and well-kept properties, but the areas surrounding it, particularly off Dwight Street, were already beginning to deteriorate into one of the seedier parts of the city. For the first couple of years, until she found a job, my mother did light housekeeping, sewing, and ironing in exchange for a rent-free room.

The arrangement was more than an even exchange. No one could argue there was anyone better in Springfield, Massachusetts, at sewing and ironing than my mother. She had strong hands, her fingers long and thick, with prominent veins and knuckles, her grasp as steady and firm as any man's. Sewing was like breathing to her, and any great sewer is, without question, also a skillful ironer — or more to the point, a presser. My mother's ironing board was always ready, with its propped-up iron, measuring cup of lukewarm water, and press cloth. A steady stream of shirts, pants, jackets, and dresses came her way for pressing as well as the seams of her homemade clothes in order to lay them flat. The pressed garments had a smooth, even look, and their collars were often stiff with starch when hung on a hanger and placed back in the closet.

One winter evening, Mrs. Alpert came into our room for a momentous announcement. Outside, it was snowing hard enough to cover the roads, sidewalks, cars, and trees with a thick blanket of soft, white crystals, like the scene so ubiquitous on old New England calendars. *I'd like to meet with you both tomorrow morning at ten o'clock. I have something very important to tell you,* she announced with a hint of both excitement and eagerness. My mother nodded, indicating that she and I would join Mrs. Alpert the next morning.

I had not yet turned five years old in the winter of 1952, but I remember that my mother appeared to be stoic about Mrs. Alpert's request. *Don't vorry, Hanele. Ve be fine,* she whispered to me, her Hungarian accent substituting the ubiquitous letter "v" for "w," and calling me *Hanele*, a Yiddish term of endearment for my name, in essence, "Little Hanna." Her face maintained its usual coolness and composure, and in a strange way, made me feel safe and protected. I believed she would always take care of everything. *Don't vorry, Hanele. Ve be fine.*

For three years, we had been part of the Alpert family, and even though I understood that the Alperts were not our relatives, I was used to being pampered and spoiled by Sarah Alpert, a widow, and her two adult sons, Arnold and Gerald. It never dawned on me to worry that our comfortable circumstances might be disrupted.

The following morning we awoke early and dressed in our room for the meeting with Mrs. Alpert. My mother made all our clothes by hand and gave a great deal of thought to how we presented ourselves. Our clothing was stylish, yet simple and subdued, with no frills or embellishments. As I look back on those early years, I realize that my mother was careful not to overstep her boundaries or put on airs that would lead anyone to think we were deliberately trying to impress them. I remember someone once saying, *Oh, look. How clean and neat and well pressed those two always look. And the little girl is so well behaved.* In those days, my mother would have been greatly satisfied by such observations.

For this important day, we were both wearing black-and-white clothes befitting a serious, sober, and almost businesslike occasion. My mother donned a white jersey-knit shoulder-padded pullover top combined with a straight black wool skirt, an outfit considerably enhanced by her broad shoulders and perfect, linear posture. Her dark brown, almost black, hair was totally pulled back from her face and pinned on the sides, revealing high cheekbones and regal, stark features, unadorned by makeup, except for red lipstick. She wore support hose to ease the circulation in her thick legs, striated with numerous bulging varicose veins, and her black, practical, wide-heeled shoes. Her gaze was always straight ahead, with her chin held up high. She was never considered pretty, but when she walked into a room, she had a dignified look that gave the impression of someone much taller than her five-foot, five-inch frame.

I wore the wool suit she had recently made, a black–and–white check-plaid pleated skirt and matching jacket with tailored collar and cuffs, and a white, pressed blouse. White wool knee socks and black Mary Jane shoes finished the outfit. My golden brown hair was combed in the fashion worn by many little girls who had recently arrived from Europe: long at the bottom but gathered at the top and rolled over like a jellyroll, secured by two long bobby pins.

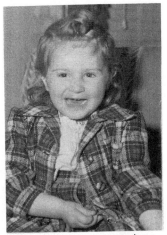

At Mrs. Alpert's house, wearing a black-and-white-check plaid suit. Photo by Kenneth Miller, American International College, Audio-Visual Department

Mrs. Alpert met us in her living room and sat us down on two of her flowered, striped-silk overstuffed chairs. She was a tall, well-built woman in her forties, with warm brown eyes, a broad smile, and short, dark hair. Standing next to her was a tall, tanned, middle-aged man whose brown hair was peppered with gray. Mrs. Alpert had a shy grin on her face as she and the man sat down together on the sofa.

Sidonia, Hanna, you remember Sam Greenberg, she said, as she turned to face the man sitting beside her. *He and I are engaged to be married, and so you both will have to move by the end of the month. My sons and I have enjoyed having you in our home, and I'll do everything I can to find you another place to live.*

I looked at my mother, stunned. *How could she think of doing this to us?* I thought to myself. *Doesn't she need us anymore?*

I could not understand why Mrs. Alpert's impending marriage meant that we could no longer live in her house. Having to move was not a first for my mother, but for me, it was a first taste of feeling rejection, of being cast out, of not belonging.

With a stern face, and showing no surprise, my mother said, *Okay. I vish you bot da best. Ve look for anoder place. Tank you for everyting.* She gazed over at me, sitting in the adjacent chair, as though to say, *Don't cry, Hanele, stay quiet. Sha.*

Even at the age of four, I had already learned to understand my mother's nonverbal cues: her clearing of her throat, her pressed lips, and her eyes staring stiffly at the floor, or sometimes staring at my face but never directly into my eyes. Aside from the look, there was no other exchange between my mother and me about leaving Mrs. Alpert's home, a pattern of behavior that we would follow for the next fifty years. She already seemed accustomed to hiding her true feelings. She skillfully acted as though leaving the only home we had ever known in America was something she had planned all along. Yet, it would be our first move since arriving in Springfield, and it could not have been an easy one for her.

Since my mother started working in 1951, I had stayed during the day with Mr. and Mrs. Steinberg, Polish Holocaust survivors who rented the floor downstairs. They had arrived in this country around the same time we did, in 1949, when Americans were celebrating the anniversary of their independence. I had grown to love them, almost as grandparents, along with their twelve-year-old son, Jerry, and their dog, Donna. My mother was usually afraid of allowing me to get too close to dogs for fear that I might be harassed or bitten. She usually admonished me as we passed a dog on the street: *Don't get so close, Hanele. Don't touch her,* but she conceded to my relationship with the Steinberg's cocker spaniel, with whom I often sparred on their linoleum kitchen floor. I remember my anxiety at the possibility of never seeing the Steinbergs or Donna again, wondering why I suddenly had to sacrifice this warm, nurturing family.

Most of all, I would miss Mrs. Alpert's two handsome adult sons. Gerald, a tall, slender young man, was prone to broad laughter as I paraded in oversized clothes and hats down an imaginary runway, the scene a precursor of my later life. His older brother, Arnold, had a slightly plumper face and form, bearing a strong resemblance to his mother, with similar dark wavy hair and a wide smile. Gerald had spent much of the time I lived at his house as a corporal in the Marine Corps fighting in the Korean War. But once he sent me a beautiful pair of peacock blue oriental silk pajamas embroidered with colorful flowers. Since I had grown so much during the year he was gone, the pajamas did not fit me when they arrived, which explains why they remain folded in a box even today, tissue paper intact, the same way they looked when I was four. Arnold was studying to be a pharmacist and had mopped floors at nearby Shankman's Pharmacy since he was ten.

I wanted to tell my mother, *Please ma, please, let's not go. Let's not leave here. I have everything I want here, older brothers, grandparents, and a dog.* But I had been trained to hold my concerns inside, not to speak out about things I wanted to say or ask, so I kept my mouth shut.

2 Hooks and Eyes

With a few exceptions . . . garments have fasteners at openings. Some, such as . . . hooks and eyes, are concealed. . . . Snaps are used where there is little strain. Hooks and eyes form a much stronger closure. Attach fasteners through holes provided for the purpose, taking over-and-over stitches that will not show on outside of garment. — "Fasteners," page 88

1998. The letter finally arrived. I sat across from my mother at her kitchen table near her gas stove, the one she had bought when we lived in our old apartment on Osgood Street, still working after forty-six years, pilot light and all. She knew by the return address on the envelope that it was from Springfield's Jewish Geriatric Services. She sensed that it contained the news she had been waiting for during the previous five years.

Hani, open it, open it. I so nerved up, I can't take it! she pleaded, sitting on the edge of her seat.

I opened the envelope quickly, ripping it on the side, the way she usually did.

It says that you made it to the top of the waiting list, ma. You're in. You have an apartment at Genesis House. Congratulations, I announced with a smile, *you're moving in next month.*

She let out a long, loud breath, *Tank Got.*

I'm glad this news makes you so happy, I said.

I was pleased that she was finally going to leave the six-room upstairs apartment in the two-family home that she had rented for the previous forty years to move to elderly housing. At age eighty-five, it had become increasingly difficult for her to negotiate the long flight of stairs. I was delighted at the thought of her moving to a new unit at ground level. But did she have the same reason for being so enthusiastic? Not really.

> *Hani, I gonna save so much money vhen I move to da substitute apartment,* she announced in a gleeful tone, showing elation about the one subject that excited her as much as sewing: saving money.
>
> *Well, ma, I hope the subsidized apartment is all that you hoped for. It'll be a lot smaller than this place, so, you know, we'll have to get rid of some of the things you really don't need.*
>
> *Dat's fine. I don't care. I ready,* she responded in her still-pronounced Hungarian accent, the English language twisted around her tongue.
>
> *All right ma. I'll come at the end of the month with my friend Paula and the movers to move you out of here and into your new place.*
>
> *Tank you, Hani. Dis is a new chapter in mine life.*

Over the next few weeks, my mother and I began to comb through her belongings, deciding which items she wanted to take to the new apartment. But we saved most of the work for moving day. Paula, the movers, and I converged on my mother's second-floor apartment like a whirlwind, throwing old musty rugs, moth-eaten fabric, used zippers, and ripped, outdated patterns into large plastic garbage bags for disposal. As we worked, we exchanged rapid-fire conversation about which pieces of furniture should be moved first. I decided to leave all the kitchen appliances right where they were, since the new apartment was equipped with its own, and arranged to take one of her two sewing machines home with me, leaving the other one to move with her to her new living quarters.

My mother was finding it hard to keep up with us despite her reasonably good physical and mental condition. She had lost sight of me when I began opening the drawers of her bedroom furniture to see whether I could lighten the load by discarding unnecessary items. There, in the middle drawer of her nightstand, I found the hundred or more pictures and faded letters and envelopes that I had seen at fleeting moments throughout my life. Many were tucked into the handmade zippered cloth bags she had begun sewing in her later years, or in plastic baggies, bunched together with elastic bands. Some were just lying in the open, not encased in any wrapping, waiting for the world to notice them, or maybe they were just waiting for me. I could not take my eyes off the long-concealed treasures that might offer personal insights into my mother's life. They were like magnets drawing me closer, hooks concealed so tightly on the inside that they baited me to uncover them.

Without flinching, but with my heart beating as though I had just run a marathon, I put handfuls of the pile into my purse and tote bag. I resisted taking all of them for fear my mother would either see me or later detect their absence. She had a sixth sense about lies and almost always knew when I was exercising that delinquent pleasure. I cringed at the thought of being discovered.

For the next two weeks, I waited to see whether she would mention that something was missing, expecting she would surely notice, but she never did. I was in the clear to start peering into those hidden thoughts and images that had taunted and beckoned me to release them from their middle-drawer confinement for more than fifty years. During the next eight years, until her

death, I led a secret life of discovery that I kept from her in a way
I doubted I could sustain.

3 Seams

A seam is the line of stitching . . . that holds two pieces of a garment together. . . . Seams can be made in different ways and with different finishes, depending on fabric, design, and purpose of garment. — "Seams and Seam Finishes," page 158

1998. Satisfied that my mother had not noticed their absence, I began to examine the old letters, envelopes, and pictures I had stolen from her drawer. I felt a surge of excitement and heightened anticipation as I removed them all from my bags and spread them out on my bedroom floor, reveling in my good fortune at having them in my possession, at long last.

My mother and I had lived alone together during my entire childhood. Along the way, by withholding salient details about her past that would have helped me to make sense of her in the present, she created a barrier between us that I could never cross. Above all, she had tried to protect us both from any pain or sorrow that could have interfered with our building content and peaceful lives. I knew that events in my mother's life had made her even more complex than she seemed. These documents, I was sure, would provide answers to questions I had held inside for many years.

Most of the letters had already developed a brownish tinge, the ink on them faded, and the folds and edges torn. They were still legible, however, and the black-and-white photos remained in excellent condition. I wished I could understand more Hungarian, German, and Yiddish, which appeared to be the languages used in the letters, but the extent of my knowledge of those languages consisted of assorted words and phrases, not enough to translate the full meaning of most of the written correspondence.

One letter stood out among them all, not only because of the simple label on the envelope, but because the writer's hybrid German, written in a kind of Yiddish style, made it relatively simple for me to translate on my own, with just a little help from a German–English dictionary. I chose it to be the first letter to tackle, confident that I could adequately interpret its story. It was in a dull-white envelope labeled in pencil in my mother's own hand in Hungarian: *Kis Etu Levele* (Little Etu's Letter). *Kis Etu*, a name I had heard in my youth and adulthood, had written to my mother, and although the original envelope was apparently lost, my mother had judged the letter important enough to hand label another one, making sure to identify the sender.

Inside, I found two documents, both written in German. One of them, a four- by seven-inch piece of graph paper, accompanied the main letter and was typewritten by an intermediary from Czechoslovakia. It read:

Dobschau, 12.11.1947 [November 12, 1947]

Greetings Fraulein!
 I am sending you a letter from your sister in Ujhel [short for Sátoraljaújhely]. It does not come directly from Hungary, since the letter was written in Hungarian, and we can only correspond in the German language, so I have translated it. Please excuse me for sending it so late, but I had forgotten about it. Send your response to me at:

Liza Dreschler, Dobsina [sic], Tscheslowakia

Enclosed on a piece of plain, fragile, eight- by eleven-inch white paper was the typewritten German translation of the letter, delayed by almost ten months.

January 22, 1947

Szidonia Perlstein
Bergen Belsen Camp
Block #L2
Dear Sidikem!!

When I learned your address, I wanted to send you a letter to explain what has happened to me. Believe me, it will interest you as much as I will be interested in everything about you.

I do not know if you knew that on July 11, 1946, I married. We were together for four months, and on November 1, 1946, unfortunately, I became a widow. My husband suddenly died, and now I am alone again. No one has returned from the family but me. Poor Joszi was killed by a bomb one day after the liberation of Budapest. My father, [Big] Etus, Saju, and Slojme are not here. And also I haven't heard anything about you.

But I think I have written enough about me. Now I'd like to hear about you. How are you? Are you healthy? What are your plans? I would very much like to see you. If we can't meet, at least send me a picture, and write me about everything that has happened to you because it is all of interest to me.

I forgot to tell you that Zszuzsi from Dámóc is engaged to a boy from Ujhel. Burech Rein is here. Dezsosz Swager also got married. He has a very pretty and nice wife. They live here in Ujhel. Dear Sidi, I beg you, if you know anything about where anyone is, write to me immediately, since it would be a shame to allow it to be forgotten.

I end my story. Believe that I have written you everything.

I kiss you repeatedly.
Your faithful sister.
Little Etu

Respond to the following address:
Widow of Szamet Salamon
S.A. Ujhel Grof Somogyi I.u.15

Once I had finished reading and translating Little Etu's words, I felt as though I had known her myself, as though I had known her for a long time. I found myself crying by the end of the second paragraph and wanting to hug her as hard as I could when I read the words *My husband suddenly died, and now I am alone again. No one has returned from the family but me.*

Although she referred to herself as *sister* in the letter, she was not my mother's sister, but her stepniece, since my mother's sister, "Big" Etu, had married her father, a widower with four children. It seemed clear, from the letter's youthful exuberance, from the gossip about young people back home and the yearning for news about other family members and my mother's life ("Are you healthy? What are your plans?"), that my mother and Little Etu were buddies. Their relationship had expanded beyond being relatives by marriage. Like young schoolgirls, they shared intimate secrets. They were as two pieces of fabric stitched together in a complete garment. While my mother was already past thirty when she left her home, a tiny hamlet in northeastern Hungary, she was unmarried, probably close in age to Little Etu, and glad to have a young friend in the nearby big city, Sátoraljaújhely (pronounced 'Sha-tor-al-ooy'-hel').

My mother rarely had close friendships during her life in America. I never even thought of her and the word "buddy" in the same sentence. It seemed alien to think of her as being close to anyone, but here was evidence to the contrary. At one time, in a different place, at a different time, and with a different attitude toward life, my mother was a young girl, with innocent friendships, crushes on boys, and giddy conversations. As I read this first letter among her as yet untranslated collection, I tried to synthesize the woman I knew as my mother, the woman who had never allowed me to gain entrance to her innermost secrets, with the woman who received this correspondence from her "faithful sister." In the process, I began to open my heart and imagination to the revelations that were to come.

By the time my mother had received this letter, she was no longer the young woman Little Etu remembered from Dámóc (pronounced 'Dah-motz'), Hungary, with whom she had enjoyed girl talk. In only three years since leaving her home, my mother had been through the most terrifying, unimaginable experiences. She had lost her family and had given birth to a child out of wedlock only months before receiving the correspondence from Little Etu. Knowing, as I did, some of the events that occurred after the letter had been written, I was certain my mother had never responded.

4 Alterations

An alteration . . . is an adjustment made in . . . [the] detail of a
garment. . . . Alterations are made for fit. . . . If you have no one
to help you with pinning and marking, you *can* do the job alone
by pinning as seems necessary and trying on repeatedly. But
it is both easier and safer with a bit of help. — "Alterations on
Finished Garments," page 11

1949. Sometimes I saw our immigration visa pictures when my
mother opened her wallet. They were filed there in the plastic
photo section among the few pictures of her grandchildren she
carried in her purse. At other times, I ran across additional copies of them among the piles of pictures in her nightstand's middle
drawer. I never paid much attention to the quickly made snapshots
taken in May of 1949 at Camp Wentorf, the Regional Resettlement
Processing Center near Hamburg, Germany. When I view them
now, the eyes and mouths, body language, clothing, and hair speak
to me of a momentous time in both our lives.

My mother had grown her hair past shoulder length, the top
portion swept up and set in a tight crimped wave, the sides pulled
severely back, and the bottom of her hair formed in another tight
wave just touching her shoulders. Wearing no makeup at all, her
face is somber and tightlipped. Her hazel eyes in the black-and-
white photo appear as dark as a moonless night, looking eerily
hypnotized. Her eyebrows are unpampered, overshadowed by her
deep-set, heavy eyelids. Her strong nose and narrow lips bring out
the leanness of her face. She wears a homemade, stone-brown,

fitted wool coat with stiff shoulder pads and a pointed collar, a patterned scarf tucked inside. Her seriousness may reflect the gravity of her passage to a new unknown world, but then again, she may just be following her own first rule of picture posing: never deliberately smile.

The photo of me reveals a twenty-one month-old toddler dressed warmly in a black wool jacket with its own attached tight-fitting turtleneck, buttoned at the shoulder and down along one side, a hand-sewn topstitch adorning the edge of the collar and the side opening. My hair is just long enough to be swept up at the top in the beginnings of the jellyroll that I would wear for the next few years. My pudgy face is serious, but my mouth is slightly open, as though to ask a question, or perhaps it is an inclination to an inevitable smile, someday.

We had been transferred to Camp Wentorf, sixty miles north of the Bergen Belsen displaced persons camp (or Camp Hohne, as the British referred to the military base that housed displaced persons) in order to process our documentation for emigration to the United States. Among the documents required: affidavits of birth, certificates of character, applications for immigration visa, and alien registration, eligibility as a displaced person, and medical certificates. It took a full two months to complete the painstaking process with multiple government officials representing various commissions, organizations, and committees that shepherded us through a maze of bureaucracy.

My mother and I were among thousands of anxious refugees at Camp Wentorf waiting for their approval to emigrate, many having born children during their time as displaced persons after the war. Years later, my mother saw a picture advertising an international conference on Jewish displaced persons that depicted a parade of new mothers walking down a tree-lined street with their babies in little white strollers. The smiles on the faces of these mothers, all former inmates of concentration camps and other survivors, seemed to signify their defiance to those who had wished them dead just a few short years before. Their defiance was attested to by the highest birthrate in the world in the few years after World War II.

She cut out the photograph, exclaiming, *Look, Hani. Dat's me an you in da picture fun Hamburg,* excitedly pointing to one of the pictured women and babies. *Do you recognize me?*

No, ma. I can't see their faces too well in the picture. They all look like you to me. I replied.

Han, I can't believe it dat you don't recognize me. I know dat I vas in dat group.

We had few of the required documents in our possession when we arrived at Camp Wentorf, but copies of my birth certificate were fairly easy to obtain. They were probably included in my file from the Bergen Belsen camp. It states in German:

Hanna Perlstein was born on August 29, 1947 at 2:30 pm in Hohne Camp [Bergen Belsen], Glyn Hughes Hospital. Father: [blank], Mother: Szidonia Perlstein, Jewish.

My mother's birth certificate, on the other hand, was much more difficult to find and would have required sending a request to the registry of her region in Hungary. The officials determined that affidavits of birth would suffice, and on March 5, 1949, while still at the Bergen Belsen displaced persons (DP) camp, she swore that she had been born in Dámóc, Hungary, on February 28, 1919. Two fellow DPs had signed a deposition affirming the truth of her statements: Andor Schwartz, born in Szabadka, Hungary, now part of Serbia, and his wife, Rozsi Kallos, born in Budapest. Neither of them had any personal knowledge of the date or place of my mother's birth. She was free to indicate any date of birth she was inclined to present, and as I would learn many years later, it was more than a slight alteration.

There were several documents that attested to my mother's good character, starting with a statement signed and stamped by the Jewish Civil Police on February 24, 1949, which stated:

> *This is to certify that Perlstein Sidonia is of good charac-*
> *ter and has never to our knowledge been convicted of any*
> *misdemeanor. She does not belong to any political party or*
> *organization that believes in the use of force to achieve its*
> *aims or purposes.*

A few days later, on February 28, the Investigations Section of the United States Displaced Persons Commission certified that its records showed:

> *No conviction under military government or German*
> *law. According to documents held by this office and personal*
> *knowledge of the person, she is of good character.*

Finally, in Wentorf, the U.S. Displaced Persons Commission certified on May 5, 1949:

> *The principal applicant and her daughter are of good*
> *character and behavior. . . . The principal applicant and her*
> *daughter are not . . . in any movement that is or has been*
> *hostile to the United States.*

Sidonia's certificate of character, issued by the Belsen police superintendent, Jewish camp, February 24, 1949

After three investigative agencies were satisfied that we were not subversives attempting to gain entry into the United States, we were allowed to move on to our physical examinations, one of the final hurdles at Camp Wentorf.

We were required to have a chest X-ray, blood tests, and a physical exam. The medical examination of visa applicants carried out by the American Foreign Service confirmed that we were examined on May 20 for evidence of such diseases as "tuberculosis" and "other loathsome or dangerous contagious" diseases, for mental conditions, such as "idiocy, imbecility, feeblemindedness, and constitutional psychopathic inferiority," in addition to "any physical defect which might affect ability to earn a living." My mother's examination revealed "bilateral varicose veins" in her legs and "flat feet," and a notation of "mastitis" of the breast, incurred in 1947 shortly after my birth. But having passed all the other tests, she was judged healthy enough for a visa. My examination, like my mother's, culminated in a note of "flat feet," and I was also cleared for emigration. The camp doctor certified on June 13 that we had been "found free of infectious diseases and DDT dusting had been carried out," to put the final stamp on any insects or vermin we may have been harboring. We had been more fortunate than some other emigrants who had not passed the medical tests and were, therefore, not allowed to leave the country.

My mother once told me the story of a man she knew who had failed one of the medical tests. A spot had been found on his chest X-ray, and he was turned away, forced to return to Bergen Belsen. Shaken by this result, he wondered how he would find the money required to make his way back to the camp. Who would help him? After being turned away by a few people, he asked my mother whether she would consider assisting him with the money he needed to return. Her answer was yes, she would give him the funds he needed on the condition that when he was able, he would pay her back. She warned him that she would not forget the debt. The man made his way back to Bergen Belsen to treat his medical problem, eventually passed the medical tests, and ultimately landed in the United States.

I once asked her many years later, *Ma, how come you had the money to help someone in that situation?* Her reply, *I alvays have some money, Hanele, alvays.*

She told me that during that time she had thought about returning to Hungary, to her little village of Dámóc, and going back to a familiar language, culture, and country — but also the country that had carried out her family's deportation. She decided she would rather take the risk of making a new home somewhere else than face her former country without those she had loved and lost.

As I sorted through the letters that I had found in my mother's drawer, I found several that disclosed the frustration as well as poignancy that marked my mother's often-futile search for those American relatives she hoped could help her. They point out that her search began soon after her liberation in 1945. This early piece of correspondence, written in Hungarian, shows her attempt initially at finding the richest cousins among her American relations, whom she had heard tales about growing up as a child in Hungary.

October 20, 1947
Beverly Hills, California
Ayin Mem Shin [Hebrew letters meaning 'may you live until 120']
Szidonia Perlstein
Bergen Belsen Camp

Dear Szidonia Perlstein,

It has been more than two years since I wrote the address of your uncle, and they wrote to you, but the letters were returned since they did not have the proper address. I called them this evening. It's not possible to talk to the husband because, unfortunately, he is too ill. They have a fur-trading store. This evening, I put your letter with your exact address in an envelope, and they will write to you. You must also write to them right away. It is important that you ask them for help since they are quite wealthy.

Send me a photo, and you can count on me.

Rabbi Nandor Friedmann

This letter must have been encouraging for my mother after having lived in a displaced persons camp for more than two years. It seemed as though she was getting closer to finding her cousins and securing the family sponsorship she desperately needed. Yet before our departure from Germany, she still had not received any contact from relatives who may have been in a position to help her make her way in the United States. On May 26, 1949, our applications for an immigrant visa were approved by the vice consul of the American Foreign Service in Hamburg. No passport or fee was required. Asked by the American Jewish Joint Distribution Committee, which helped to resettle Jewish Holocaust survivors, whether she could identify anyone in the United States who could act as her sponsor, my mother was forced to say that she could not. So, she took the offer of the International Refugee Organization to settle in Springfield, Massachusetts. Her visa listed her intention to join the *Committee for New Americans, 145 State St, Springfield, Massachusetts*. Her intended occupation: *Seamstress*.

The USS *General R. L. Howze*, a ship named in honor of an American general who received the Distinguished Service Medal for his World War I service, had already seen its share of action during World War II. It had made eleven voyages to the Pacific during 1944 and 1945 carrying troops, supplies, and Japanese prisoners. Acquired by the U.S. Army Transportation Service (renamed USAT) in 1948, it was commissioned as the USAT *General R. L. Howze*, assigned to transport war refugees to new points of destination.

The *Howze* would be our vehicle to a new country, an escape from the black shadows of a lost family and of unfulfilled desires. For my mother, the destination did not necessarily bring dreams of a bright future, but of a safe place where a mother and child could live. Leaving the port of Bremerhaven around June 23, 1949, we arrived at the port of New York on July 3 after a rough crossing and severe bouts with seasickness. My mother spoke of it many times during my childhood, recalling the dizzy rocking and pungent smells of the ship and the many hours that we, like the rest of the passengers, spent vomiting.

Here are the possessions my mother brought with her on the ship, many purchased from the black market with the compensation she earned for sewing work during her four-year stay at the Bergen Belsen displaced persons camp: six settings of Rosenthal china, an assortment of brown-and-white enameled pots and pans, silver–plated candelabra, two goose-down blankets, pictures taken during her years at Bergen Belsen, sewing supplies, and a Köhler console sewing machine. These few things, in their own way, defined everything that was most important to her: kitchen and dining items that were essential to establishing a home; candelabra to light candles on the Jewish "Shabbos"; sewing supplies and a sewing machine, which had made her life's vocation and avocation possible; and pictures representing memories of a period of her life that, in many ways, formed the basis of her future.

As we arrived in New York with hundreds of other war refugees, my mother had never been so alone. At the time, the only person she knew in America was me, the twenty-two-month-old child at her side. We spent two days at a hotel processing more documents and then took the three-hour train trip to Springfield, arriving on July 5, 1949. My mother had two dollars in her pocket.

The long-awaited response from her rich relatives came only four months after our arrival at New York harbor. Written in Hungarian with a firm hand, using a blue fountain pen on formal stationary, my mother's uncle's wife wrote:

November 9, 1949
Beverly Hills, California

Dear Szidonia,
   It is I who has to answer your letter. It looks as though no

one can avoid her destiny. My husband has been in the hospital for eighteen months, incurably ill. It seems, my dear, not only you and European Jews are going through great difficulties, but also those who are here. He was a wealthy young man, but now he has been half dead for eighteen months. My son is still going to school and won't be able to help us for many more years. Now I have to earn the living. You are still young, and God will surely show you the way. If you can, please send pictures of you and your daughter. I will forward your letter to my husband. Unfortunately, I don't think he will remember you because his condition is so severe. Greetings and I wish you a lot of luck.

With lots of love,
Elsa

As I read the translation of this letter, I realized that as an American Jew, perhaps a naturalized citizen, this relation was not able to comprehend the torture my mother had experienced. "It looks as though no one can avoid her destiny. . . . It seems, my dear, that not only you and European Jews are going through great difficulties, but also those who are here." In her own misery, she had equated my mother's loss with her own and could not reach out to someone who had been affected by events as heinous as have ever been encountered on the face of the earth.

I could envision the bitter disappointment my mother felt upon reading her cousin's letter. Her efforts at making a connection with the wealthy relations she had heard about during her childhood were summarily crushed. With no news about any other relatives in her new country, she must have wondered whether her fate was to live in a land where she would be totally bereft of family. The deep sorrow and fear she experienced must have been almost unbearable.

No one but she was privy to the information contained in this cousin's letter, as was the case with the rest of the letters I found. She kept them inside her in a portion of her soul that she may have visited from time to time, but she had a daughter for whom she was responsible. She would forge ahead, continue to search for relatives, and try to face her destiny.

5 Machine Stitching

The key to success in stitching *any* fabric with *any* kind of thread lies in your sewing machine. . . . Your machine will stitch perfectly if you are particular about certain points in its use . . . a clean machine, thread and needle chosen to suit the fabric . . . pace of stitching steady and even. — "Machine Stitching," pages 114 and 115

Springfield, Massachusetts, was a large city by New England standards. Situated in the western portion of the state, along the banks of the Connecticut River, its population of 160,000 in the early 1950s made it the fourth largest in New England. Famous for its manufacture of firearms, such as the historic Springfield Rifle, it was still a bustling place in the late 1940s and 1950s, when an immigrant could find work in its factories, retail stores, and industrial infrastructure.

My mother had only attained a sixth-grade education in her homeland of Hungary and had no professional training or technical knowledge. The most marketable skill she possessed was sewing. It took almost two years for her to find a job, which came possibly through a connection of Mrs. Alpert's. Or it may have been someone at the Springfield Committee for New Americans who took on the difficult task of helping a single woman with a child, possessing negligible English, little education, and no transportation. Maybe someone pointed out an ad in the *Springfield Daily News* like this: *Sewing machine operators needed, piecework on women's dresses, no prior experience required.* One way or another, sometime in the spring of 1951, my mother started work at the Victoria Dress Corporation on William Street in the south end of Springfield, next door to the enticing fragrances of Frigo's Italian cheeses and meats.

The company made everyday ladies garments, usually a print jersey silk dress with a matching short jacket in the style of the day. The garments would arrive as cut-out pattern pieces that had to be sewn together to produce the finished product. My mother had learned to sew in her small Hungarian village, where every female member of her family — her mother and three sisters — were expert sewers. It was one of the numerous ways the family earned its income. As she told me many times in her self-effacing manner: *Hanele, I not such a good sewer, not as good as my sister Szeren. I should be half as good as her.*

But here in the United States, in Springfield, Massachusetts, she was a sewing sharpshooter. Mr. Podell, the owner of the Victoria Dress Corporation, put her on a machine that first day just to see what she could do, and she was hired on the spot. His heart must have jumped in his chest to see my mother fly through the pieces of fabric with such speed and accuracy. She started doing piecework at a few cents for each piece of garment, and eventually she was paid hourly. After a few years, she worked her way up the ranks to become the forewoman of the shop, with an annual salary. It was a job she would hold for more than fourteen years.

A dashing yet avuncular older man with white hair, Mr. Podell was secure in his station in life, always wearing an expensive dark suit and tie and driving his flashy, black Chrysler New Yorker. His garment business had been good to him and to his family, and, to his credit, he wanted to use his wealth to help refugees who had recently come to Springfield to seek new lives after World War II. He understood my mother's situation immediately. A woman with a small child and no family would need a protector who could ensure that she would be safe and comfortable, meet her basic needs of food and shelter, and most of all, treat her nonjudgmentally. Mr. Podell was that person for my mother and me.

I am certain that my mother viewed Mr. Podell as a surrogate father from the very beginning. She respected him for his wisdom about human nature and his knowledge of American society and culture. He taught her to develop a tough outer skin and to shield herself against the hatred and jealousy she would experience in America, and maybe even at the Victoria Dress Corporation.

Sometimes I saw him take her aside at the factory to firmly, yet kindly, explain his expectations for the latest dress line, confident that she would explicitly understand his instructions despite her lack of fluency in the English language. When we moved from the Alperts, it was he who arranged for a new blond Hollywood bed, with its low legs and upholstered cream-colored vinyl headboard, that constituted my only bedroom furniture.

My mother and her mainly Italian co-workers labored on two floors in the old industrial building that housed the Victoria Dress Corporation. The male steam pressers worked on the first level, sweat dripping down their faces as they monotonously lifted up the heavy top layer of their presses and then plunged it down again on each garment, emitting a powerful burst of steam. Sometimes I would go upstairs to the second floor, where wall-to-wall sewing machines and their female operators sat amid mounds of fabric pieces. The sound of sewing machines whirring, scissors squeaking, spools of thread spinning, and voices buzzing filled the room like an urban musical symphony.

My mother began to make friends with her fellow operators and learned the English language with a particular mixed Hungarian and Italian flavor. The Victoria Dress Corporation became a place where she gained respect for her skill and gradually earned enough income to make a decent living. I would watch her as she gave instructions to the sewing machine operators about a particular dress line and as she responded to the waving hands of the sewers. To a shouted question like, *Over here, Sidonia, can you help me set in this zipper?* she responded *Okay, Carmela, I be right dere to help you. Ve can do it togeder,* as she walked over to Carmela's station and leaned over to examine the situation.

Having a working mother became a way of life for me. Watching her in action on the factory floor, once she had "made it" to forewoman, in command of everything and everyone, became the main reason I was proud of her.

During her years at the shop, my mother and I were invited to workers' homes in Springfield's south end or in nearby Thompsonville, Connecticut. We spent some lazy summer days in the green, well-kept backyards of these workmates, sipping lemonade on their outdoor wicker furniture. I remember thinking that someday I would like to live in a similar place. A lawn and backyard would always be a dream for me, one that my mother would never attain for us. Although I now realize that some of my mother's co-workers were immigrants themselves, as a child I believed that owning a home with a yard was reserved for those born in America.

Not all the workers at the shop developed friendships with my mother. One notable exception was the foreman at the Victoria Dress Corporation, an Italian-American named Johnny, or *Chonny,* as my mother called him. I saw him frequently as I waited for my mother in the small office near the entrance of the factory, partitioned off from the rest of the first floor. He was a tall, beefy-looking man, with a mop of dark hair falling in a disheveled curl over his forehead. He spoke in a loud, gruff voice, usually muffled by a cigarette hanging out of his large mouth, like a car wreck hovering over a cliff. Johnny never pretended any fondness for my mother, speaking to her only when necessary, and then with a look of disdain. He was feeling the pressure of competition from someone, a recent foreigner who had gained favor with the boss and had considerable talent in the sewing business.

One day, as I sat in the office, a preteen at the time, he approached me and asked, *So, your name is Hanna, is it?*

> *Yes, I* replied, *it is,* wondering where the conversation was going.
>
> *So, how do you spell that?*
>
> *It's spelled H-a-n-n-a.*
>
> *Well, that's not the right way to spell your name, it should have an "h" at the end,* he commented with consternation.
>
> *I'm sorry, but that's how it's spelled. It's on my birth certificate. That's how I've always spelled it,* I retorted, my defenses up and my adrenaline flowing.
>
> *You know, you're in America now,* he said with a hint of contempt. *You're not in Europe. You have to act like an American. You should be spelling your name the American way.*
>
> *Well, last time I looked, I was an American,* I said, ending the conversation, *and it's a free country.*

That was one of the few times as a child I realized that not everyone accepted my mother and me as equals in American society. The influx of Jewish refugees after World War II had created resentment among some Americans who were trying to make a living as blue-collar workers. The fact that my mother was a woman and a Jew could have been a further in-your-face blow to Johnny and his masculinity.

Although many women returned to their homes as traditional housewives and mothers after their stint as factory and industrial workers during the war effort in the 1940s, my mother, like many immigrant women, had to work to make ends meet. In her case, it was the only income available to support our little family. Observing my mother's solitary life, I wondered whether other men, besides Johnny, resented her self-reliance and independent spirit as well.

6 Interfacing

An interfacing is an extra piece of fabric placed between a facing and the outer fabric of a garment. Its purpose is to reinforce and add body and often crispness to the faced area and edge. It improves appearance and preserves shape . . . on an open neckline, stop stitching before point where it would show on outside. — "Interfacing," pages 108 and 111

Photo of the author in back of the Osgood Street apartment block, 2006

My mother and I left the Alperts and moved to the apartments at 64–68 Osgood Street, still in the north end of Springfield but not nearly as grand as the owner-occupied houses on Brookline Avenue. Osgood Street generally suffered from the inattention of absentee landlords or from the poor families who owned their own homes but lacked the means to invest in their maintenance. It was a ramshackle, deteriorating side street, but it was a fairly safe area, where the rents were affordable for an immigrant making minimum wage. *You vill be happy here, Hanele. You vill see*, my mother consoled me as we moved into our new place. *You vill meet oder children your age.*

Although I said nothing in response, I was frightened by the large structure of an apartment building after the warmth of a two-family home. The building held only thirty-two units, but to a five-year-old, it seemed as though it would devour me.

The four-story building stood near the corner of Dwight Street and Osgood, just beyond the Esso gas station. Constructed in the 1920s, it had a reddish-brown brick facade with white concrete squares dotting the corners of each window. Deteriorating wooden porches jutted out from the back at every level, serving as fire escapes, supports for clotheslines, and the location of the chute leading to the garbage incinerator in the basement. Our porch, leading out from the kitchen door, also revealed the back doors of the three other neighbors in our section of the third floor: the Levins, the Harrises, who were displaced Brooklynites whose steadfast devotion to the Brooklyn Dodgers I adopted, and an elderly couple whose names I have long forgotten who invited us in for tea and presented us with their homemade oil painting of a tranquil seaside village. It still adorns my office wall today.

I became accustomed to climbing the three wooden flights of the front stairway, often smelling the foul odor of the mouse mortuary that existed beneath its treads. Our apartment was one of the larger units at 64 Osgood Street, with a living room big enough to hold a sewing machine and supplies, as well as a sofa and chairs, plus two bedrooms. Our kitchen table doubled as a surface to cut patterns. I missed the close family setting we had left on Brookline Avenue, but I became immersed in a new kind of family: *di grine* (pronounced 'green-eh,' meaning 'the greenhorns').

Di grine was the Yiddish term for the community of Holocaust survivors and their children. They were "green" newcomers who were not yet assimilated into American life and culture. Outsiders. Their backgrounds varied from chemists and engineers to farmers and tradespeople; from those with urban, cultural upbringings to those with rural, uneducated, and humble origins. In another place or at another time, they would probably never have associated with one another, but in America, on Osgood Street and the surrounding area, they clung to one another as only those who have shared similar life-altering experiences can do. The bonds between them grew from the understanding that each one was a surviving ember of the smoldering flames that had consumed their families and ripped them from their homelands.

Between the ages of five and eight, *di grine* were my whole world. I rarely moved out of their sphere of influence. I lived among them, went to school with them, ate with them, played with them, and observed them. America to me was six blocks of Dwight Street, from Calhoun to Ringgold Street, where *di grine* conducted the daily life tasks of their universe.

I did not know the stories of *di grine,* their specific countries of origin, their wartime experiences, what their lives were like before they came to Springfield, how they felt about one another, or their feelings as immigrants in a strange new land. Through a child's eyes, they seemed a happy lot to me, frequently smiling, telling amusing Yiddish stories, and celebrating as a whole community, with abundant food and drink even small occasions, like a five-year-old's birthday. Like all children in an adult world, I accepted them at face value and considered them, in many ways, my extended family. So much so that I felt at liberty to meander from one apartment to another, often smelling the chicken schmaltz rendered on the stove in one apartment or watching potato kreplach pinched together before being thrown into the boiling pot in another or the cabbage stuffed and rolled with meat and rice in the next. I tasted many European Jewish culinary delights in the numerous kitchens on the Osgood Street block.

The members of *di grine* were mainly Polish, with some Hungarians and Germans and a few from other Central and Eastern European countries. But the Yiddish language, in myriad dialects, united them. Born in the exile of the Middle Ages, with its amalgam of Germanic, Slavic, and Hebrew overtones, Yiddish allowed them to communicate with ease and helped them to feel at home in a culture from which they were mostly excluded. Except among very close friends, the adults, most of whom were under forty, referred to one another respectfully by the formal "Mr." or "Mrs." From the moment we moved to the street, my mother was referred to as "Mrs." Perlstein, no matter her marital status.

Left to right, William Citron, Sidonia, Pola Fuchs, Leon Smolarz, and Sam Fuchs, around 1952

Di grine included all the characters who populate any small community. They had their share of socialites, those who knew everyone, coordinated social events, acted as matchmakers, and passed along all the latest gossip. Another group, the cardplayers, comprised mainly men, but also some women, who took their games seriously and played for nickel bets. I can still recall their deadpan faces, eyes narrowed to slits, dragging on a cigarette as they peered over their cards, either staring down at the card table or straight ahead, bluffing about an unlucky draw or the sure winner in their possession.

The sultry femme fatale was younger than most of them. Her long, dark wavy hair surrounded her chiseled face, which bore deep-red lipstick, rouge, and dark eyebrows. She often wore low-cut dresses and tight knit pullover sweaters that showcased her full breasts and narrow waist. I thought she was beautiful.

The biggest subgroup among *di grine* was the married couples with one or two children, rarely three. A few single men looking for spouses were sprinkled among the group in the early days. My mother and I did not fit into any of these groupings, yet my identification with them was as strong as, or perhaps stronger than, with any community of which I have ever been a part.

Often, my mother and I would stroll down Dwight Street and stop at Klibanoff's Delicatessen for a corned beef sandwich and kosher dill pickle. Just a few doors down we entered Ruby's Market, where the owner, Ruby himself, and Lena Hutt, one of *di grine*, greeted us with their white aprons and provided personal service as we shopped for our week's groceries. When we were finished, we walked a few more blocks to Magaziner's Bakery and ordered a couple of cupcakes and a half loaf of seedless rye bread, freshly sliced before our eyes.

Crossing the street, we landed at Shankman's Pharmacy to purchase a bottle of aspirin or a tube of toothpaste and thenwalked

At the corner of Osgood and Dwight Streets, around 1957.
The author sports a "homemade" short set; Sidonia wears a
striped cotton dress that she created.

north a little way on Dwight Street to Chernick's Kosher Meat
Market. There, Mr. Chernick stood behind his butcher-block table
surrounded by his assorted meat knives, deftly slicing and chop-
ping cuts of chicken and beef, his white apron streaked with blood.
My mother often ordered a whole chicken cut into eight pieces or
sometimes just wings for a chicken fricassee, which was a misno-
mer since it did not contain the cream of the nonkosher variety.

Gefelt es dir der fligl, Chanele? asked Mr. Chernick, using "Chanele,"
a variation of Hanele but beginning with a guttural sound, his wide
smile on his extremely round face beaming down at me.

 *Yeah, I like chicken wings a lot. The leg and the wing, those are
my favorite parts,* I responded.

 Outside Chernick's, a group of men usually stood talking
together in Yiddish, their faces and hands animated in discussion

as though daring one another to come up with the answer to some esoteric philosophical question. *Nu?* ("Well?" or "So?"), I overheard them saying, coaxing the responder to provide them with some weighty, thought-provoking reply.

Soon after moving in, my mother and I were invited to our initial social event — a birthday party for my first best friend, Shirley Horowitz, who was turning five and who lived one flight down on the second floor.

Mrs. Per-il-shtine, vill you and Chanele come to Sheerley's party? Mrs. Horowitz asked as we met on the front stairs.

Yes, Mrs. Horovitz, ve vill be dere. Tank-a-you, my mother replied, looking down at me, her mind already racing to determine what she would sew for me to wear.

We attended Shirley's birthday party and many other events after that, but I always viewed my mother and me as being on the outside of the outsiders. We were an odd pair among *di grine.* Although she sometimes went through the motions of attending social events and hosted a few birthday parties for me in our Osgood Street apartment, my mother preferred to keep to herself. Card playing was something she had always shunned, as though it were a silly way to occupy time. *Cards, dey not for me. I not interested in such games,* she would say when I asked why she did not play.

Knowing that my mother was one of the few single women in the community, the matchmakers tried to pair her with some of the bachelors among *di grine,* but she would have none of it, refusing any of their overtures. At different times during my childhood, I asked her, *Will you ever get married, ma?*

Oy, Hanele, who vants to cook an clean for a man? It's too much trouble, she would invariably reply with a solemn face. I remember feeling disappointed that she felt men were such a bother. Her attitude made it certain that I would never have a father figure in my life. I began to feel a growing resentment of my mother's disdain for men and of her seeming contentment at living a life of solitude.

Why can't she be more like everybody else, play cards or plan activities, or maybe just behave like she was a real member of the group, instead of being off by herself? I ruminated. And hoping for a father like the other kids, I felt different and ashamed of both my mother and myself. It never crossed my mind that perhaps her negative expressions about men and her self-seclusion were her way of protecting herself from emotional pain.

When *di grine* formed a social organization in the early 1950s called Club Hatikvah, incorporating the Hebrew word for "hope," we attended some of their events. The parties featured music, dancing, food, and drink. People often brought their children, and I enjoyed the company of my friends among *di grine*, many of whom were my schoolmates at the Lubavitcher Yeshiva School and playmates from Osgood Street. One evening, when I was about eight, my mother went alone to a Club Hatikvah gathering, leaving another member of *di grine* to stay with me. When my mother returned, I saw her sitting hunched over at the kitchen table, her head cupped in her hands, muttering to herself. She was visibly unnerved, or *nerved up,* as she would say, but there was no weeping.

What's wrong ma, did something bad happen tonight? I asked, lightly touching her hand.

I okay, Hanele, I fine, she responded, not willing or capable of telling me what had really happened.

But ma, something made you upset. You don't usually look this way.

With a scornful gaze, she slowly looked up at me and said, *Somevon call me a name. Some jerk call me a name.*

A man had offended her, although I never knew exactly what he had said. At the time, I thought she surely must have done something to provoke the matter, but looking back, I can imagine the slur that must have been hurled at her. I realize now that the crucible of the Holocaust had not changed the behavior norms of a small few of *di grine* who may have looked disparagingly upon an unmarried woman with a child.

From that night on, my mother avoided attending most Club Hatikvah functions, while I secretly envied my friends who were still able to attend.

In the early 1950s, during the time we were assimilating into the Osgood Street neighborhood, my mother continued to search for relatives in America, having abandoned her pursuit of the wealthy ones in Beverly Hills. I discovered the following letter she received during that time, written in Yiddish using the Hebrew alphabet, which typified such letters.

[Postmarked March 30, 1950]

Miss Perlstein,

I asked you about Andor Perlstein and Lina and Regina. I have written to the Morgen Zhurnal [a New York Yiddish daily] *to put an announcement in the paper, and I looked in the telephone book, but I have not yet reached them. The people you are looking for — write quickly — should I look for them in New York, in the Bronx, or Brooklyn? Is this a married person or not? What is their occupation? There are some possibilities, so perhaps you will discover your family and acquaintances.*

Who brought you to America? With whom are you

*there in Springfield? What are your sponsors' names? Write
everything if possible, better in Yiddish; if not, Hungarian
is also good.*

A happy, kosher Pesach [Passover],
Rabbi Yitzkhak Halevi Klein

Soon, my mother found a few cousins in New York, perhaps
through the assistance of the rabbi who had helped her in the
search, including the Lina and Regina mentioned in the letter.
They were my grandmother's first cousins, who had come to the
United States in the 1920s and settled in the Bronx, where they
lived in small tenements with their families. My mother and I took
many train excursions from Springfield to New York City during
the decade of the 1950s to visit them, along with another cousin
nearby who had survived the war.

My mother did not seem to care any longer about the financial
help that could have been provided by wealthy relations. Instead,
these relatives, most of whom she had either never met before or
had known only as a small child in her homeland, provided her
with a semblance of familial nurturing and compassion, perhaps
reminding her of her parents' generation. She could be natural and
open with them, unburden herself of the tragedy and heartbreak
festering inside her. I saw a softer side of my mother during the
visits to New York, which I always looked forward to with great
eagerness.

Back on Osgood Street, my mother was a proud woman, a
quality that did not always work in her favor. She was proud of her
sewing skills and how she could run a household, work long hours,
and raise a child by herself at the same time. Her pride may have
appeared to others as disdain or aloofness. She was often described
as the "tall woman," in part because she was taller than most of

the *di grine,* who were generally a short group of people, but also because of her neck, outstretched in pride. Her demeanor made it clear to our neighbors that they should keep their questions about her past relationship, the one that resulted in her child, to themselves. Only a few who formed a true friendship with her may have broken through her iron fortress to ask the questions that no one else would dare to ask. Even then, she may have divulged only partial truths.

Pride may have kept my mother sane or insulated her from the brutal world, but it also separated us from the rest of the members of our community and from each other, or so it seemed to me.

My resentment of her progressed into a hatred that tortured and haunted me. It permeated every bit of my body, gnawing at me, yet I could not shed it.

I sometimes imagined that my real parents had given me away to this mother because they were unable to provide for me, or maybe she had somehow stolen me from them. We did not look much alike, I reasoned — me with my golden brown hair, green eyes, and tall, ectomorphic body, and her with her dark brown hair, hazel eyes, and angular, thick-skinned, bigger-boned form. Perhaps she was not my real mother after all.

At the same time, she was the only person in my life whose face I saw every day and whose voice I heard in my sleep. I did not have anybody else to care or provide for me, who gave me safety and showed me love. Of course, I loved her even as I hated her. For a long time, I was trapped in this struggle with my emotions about the single person in the world who was my family.

7 Backing

Backing serves a number of purposes, but is never a finish. . . . In certain designs . . . backing preserves the silhouette when outside fabric does not have enough body. . . . In general, backing gives body where it may be missing. . . . . The backing must enhance, not interfere with, the outer fabric. — "Backing or Underlining," page 18

Sidonia is not a name you hear very often in the United States. I often wonder why I did not ask my mother about the origins of her unusual name, spelled S-z-i-d-o-n-i-a in Hungarian. Recently, as I searched for the meaning and roots of the name, I learned of several Princesses Maria Sidonia who were members of the royal lineages of Saxony and of the Austro-Hungarian Empire. Then, I ran across a copy of William Meinhold's *Sidonia the Sorceress* online at the Harvard Law Library. Perhaps my grandmother had read this story, published in the late nineteenth century, about the fabled sorceress, Sidonia, a beautiful rich girl betrayed by several princes of Pomerania, preventing her from marrying her lover. She vows never to marry and to carry out revenge against the House of Pomerania for scorning her.

Sidonia also stems from the ancient Phoenician word referring to a cloth of fine linen. "Sidon" was the name of the northernmost region cited as part of the original land of Canaan in the Old Testament, and later a Phoenician port city noted for its industry and commerce. The name forms a perfect pairing with my mother's unusual Hebrew name, Shasha, which may have its roots in the word *shesh* meaning 'six' but also refers to a cloth of fine linen in ancient Hebrew. Her mother and father may have decided that their sixth and last child should bear a distinctive, proud, and exceptional name.

My mother had vivid and frequent dreams about events that occurred in her past, but almost never about her present. Starting from the age of five, I could count on hearing about the previous night's dream, most often when we sat down to eat dinner. It was through these dreams that I heard tales of my mother's idyllic childhood in the little village of Dámóc, a town of only two hundred house numbers in Zemplén, a county near the border of northeastern Hungary and Czechoslovakia, now Slovakia, at the foothills of the Carpathian Mountains.

As she described the town, it was not a *shtetl* in the usual sense of the Yiddish term, referring to a small central or eastern European farming village with a substantial Jewish population. Many European Jews before the mid-twentieth century lived in vibrant communities with other agrarian Jews, practicing, and often celebrating, their Jewishness within the larger Christian culture. Always fearful of sudden pogroms at the hands of Christian leaders or soldiers, resulting in the loss of life and livelihood, *shtetl* Jews lived a proud but cautious existence, aware of the dangers lurking around them. On the contrary, Dámóc was a testament to how a group of only five Jewish families could live in peace together with hundreds of Greek Orthodox Catholics for more than a century.

Hanele, I vas born on da old part of da main street. Ve had a very Jewish, simple life in Dámóc. All da Catolic people vere our neighbors. Ve never felt dey vere against us, she remarked on more than one occasion.

You mean you never felt like they looked at you as though you were different because you were Jewish, ma? I asked.

Vell, ve knew ve vere different. Ve didn't go to dere church, and ve vere excused from Catolic studies, even dough ve stayed to learn dem anyvay. No, ve don't feel dat vay. Dey vere perfect to us, her hand raised in the okay sign.

I nodded. *Yeah, it sounds like you and they were good friends growing up together.*

As I grew older and began to read historical literature and watch television accounts of anti-Semitism in Europe over many centuries, I found my mother's stories of her childhood hard to believe. If Dámóc did truly exist, it must have been far away from the rest of Europe, I thought.

But I listened to her stories of Dámóc, captivated by descriptions of life in the small farming community and the richness of family and extended family life. She told me about raising chickens and geese and a few cows so familiar to the family that they were given pet names, as though they were dogs or cats. I heard about schoolyard games, playing ball with her sisters and brother and of friendships with her Catholic schoolmates. Stories abounded of planting apple and plum trees in the backyard of her house, of learning to sew at a Singer sewing machine from her sisters and mother, and of bringing crops to market.

One of my favorite stories relates to Easter time in the tiny village. Every Easter, each Christian family prepared its holiday feast and placed the sumptuous meal inside a basket. The basket was then covered with a cloth adorned with the most festive and colorful needlepoint of the year. Before taking this basket to the village priest for his blessing, each family brought it to my grandmother, known for her expertise in needlepointing, who diplomatically pronounced each one more beautiful than the next.

My mother relayed these events of her childhood and young adulthood with a sense of urgency, as though by telling me she were not only confirming that they had really happened to her, but also because she knew she was the only remaining witness who could recount them. I came to memorize these stories, particularly those of her family. When I thought of them, it felt as though I were in a time machine transporting me back to the early twentieth century.

JewishGen, the comprehensive Jewish genealogy website, indicates that my mother's parents, Hani Klein and Simon Perlstein, were married in the wine-producing town of Károlyfalva, Zemplén County, Hungary, on June 25, 1895. After her marriage, according to my mother, Hani moved away from her family's home and wine business in Károlyfalva to live with her husband and his family in Dámóc, thirty miles away. Simon's father, Marton, and before him, his grandfather David, had lived in Dámóc for perhaps a century before his marriage to Hani.

When he was eighteen years old, a few years before their wedding, Simon spent nine months in America. He returned to Dámóc disillusioned with the difficult lives of immigrants in New York City and by what he perceived to be the erosion of Jewish traditions and religious observance in America. My mother laughed when she recalled my grandmother's teasing about her husband's American sojourn, saying, *It vas so funny vhen my moder used to say my fader last as long in America as he did in his moder's boykh* [belly].

It has crossed my mind more than once that if Simon had stayed in America, he could have avoided what happened fifty years later. By now, many of his descendents, the offspring of his children and their children's children, would be living in the United States, Israel, or perhaps in all corners of the world, contributing in their own special way to the earth. Instead, the task was left only to my mother and me.

Although Hani was fluent in German, and both Hani and Simon were conversant in Yiddish, my mother's parents spoke only Hungarian at home with their family. Hani was a traditional Jewish mother who cooked, tended her garden, sewed, and kept the household in order. My grandfather's occupation varied from owning a tavern and bowling alley to being a shopkeeper. His main source of income, however, seems to have stemmed from his role as a *soykher* (tradesman or dealer). He, along with his children, were in the business of ensuring that the crops grown in Dámóc, like wheat, corn, and sunflower seeds, secured a fair price when brought to market in Sátoraljaújhely or Sárospatak. It was through their trading enterprise that the Perlsteins of Dámóc guaranteed their economic necessity and thus survival in their tiny village.

Simon and Hani had six children together. I heard about them from my mother this way:

Szeren was the oldest child. She was brilliant and intuitive, surrounded by books written by Hungary's most famous novelists and poets, like Mor Jokai, Janos Arany, and Sandor Petofi. She was gifted at everything she set her mind to. No one in Dámóc could surpass her sewing talent. She spent many hours at the family's Singer sewing machine, creating dresses, aprons, scarves, and shirts for the family and for the rest of the villagers. Her wisdom was acknowledged as one of the keenest in the region, and she provided advice and counsel to political and social leaders. She could talk her way out of anything. My mother would say, *She could have been president.*

Margit was the intellectual. She read books more for the sake of knowledge than for pleasure. She was the only one of the children to attend classes in the nearby city of Sátoraljaújhely, possibly at one of the secondary schools where Jewish students could learn a secular curriculum as well as Jewish studies, thereby securing the opportunity to achieve higher education, just as their non-Jewish counterparts had. Her parents' reservations on religious grounds about sending one of their daughters to a school outside their village were overcome by Margit's undeniable intellect and her voracious desire to learn. She died as a teenager of the Spanish Flu after World War I, and her parents never forgave themselves for allowing their child to leave Dámóc every day and be exposed to disease in the big city.

Etel was the stable one. She was everyone's confidante, the trusted sibling and friend who never betrayed a secret. She would patiently listen to everyone's personal story of woe. She also excelled at sewing and joined with the other girls to create everyday and special-occasion clothes.

Dezso was the rascal. The only male sibling, he was daring and clever, an adventurer willing to take risks to enhance the finances of his family. As an adolescent, he continued his orthodox Jewish studies in the great learning institutions of Maramoros Sziget, farther east into the Carpathian Mountains. As a young adult, he was embroiled in several schemes to smuggle contraband goods over the Czechoslovakian border. As a result of the Treaty of Trianon at the end of World War I, the vanquished and sprawling Austro-Hungarian Empire lost much of its former lands and grandeur. Nearby towns such as Pribenik became part of the new independent country of Czechoslovakia, and papers and permits were required for people and products to cross the border into and out of Hungary. Dezso preferred to ignore the new geographical configuration and secretly found his way across the boundary lines to obtain goods and supplies. He was arrested more than once, and Szeren, his fast-talking sister, was sent to advocate for his release. Ultimately, after one-too-many such escapades, he could no longer return home and remained in hiding in Budapest and later in Nyiregyháza.

Laura was the beautiful and delicate one. Fussy about what she ate, she often picked at her food and sometimes even refused to eat the family meal. She had ardent male admirers, but due to her strict orthodox Jewish upbringing, she never encouraged their companionship. She also was proficient in hand and machine sewing.

These stories about my mother's family were enthralling, but the people in them remained unreal to me, just as the terrible stories that followed would, even though interspersed with these happy ones. For many years, I thought my distance from these "tales" came from the dispassionate manner in which they were told. If my mother had flinched even once over a family lost, cried just once, looked clearly into my eyes just once, then maybe they would have been more tangible. But she never did.

My mother was the last of Simon and Hani Klein Perlstein's children, born when Hani was already forty-one years old and Simon was forty-four. She seemed to me to have inherited qualities that were an amalgam of those of her sisters and brother: cleverness, staunch independence, sewing talent, disdain for authority, and stubbornness.

8 True Bias

True bias is the true (45 degree) diagonal across a square of fabric, cutting exactly in half the right angle formed by the lengthwise and the crosswise grains. — "Bias," page 25

I never learned to sew. I never asked my mother to teach me anything about the sewing machine, its parts, or how to thread it. Nor can I hand stitch a torn seam, darn socks, or even sew buttons. In my partial defense, my mother never offered to give me lessons. Instead, she was perfectly content to retain sole custody of the sewing talent in our family.

As is true in all the great fashion houses, my mother had a favorite model to display her creations: me. I was usually not a very patient or enthusiastic model, tired of standing up for long periods while she fitted pieces of a garment to my body or measured a hemline. During the years that my mother worked at the Victoria Dress Corporation, I was not only the beneficiary of most of her sewing at home, but in a way I was her ambassador to the world, the personification of Sidonia Perlstein's fashion prowess and intense passion for creative design. But, more than that, I represented an extension of her family, her hard work, and her beliefs about how a child should act and look.

Hanele, can't you stand up straight? Vhy can't you put your shoulders back? I gonna have a crooked hem if you don't stand up straight, she would shout up at me from her place at my feet on the floor.

You know, ma, I've been standing for so long. I just can't wait until you're finished already. I must have responded this way a thousand times, with a level of impatience unchanged from childhood into adulthood.

> *Okay, den, I don't care. You can vear it dat vay.*
> *Ma, you're right. See, I'm standing up straight.*
> *Dat's-a-right. You smart,* she responded using two of

her most common remarks.

When she was not sitting at the machine, fitting, or hand stitching, my mother could often be found leaning over the kitchen table cutting and marking pieces of patterns for skirts, dresses, blouses, shorts, jackets, vests, or pants. She would closely examine each piece of fabric, not only with her eyes but also with her fingers, to determine the lengthwise and crosswise grains, her face transfixed as though engrossed in deep cerebral reflection. She was careful to place the pattern on the fabric exactly so that it aligned with the true bias, the diagonal line that runs midway through the right angle formed by the two grains. Her precise use of any pattern, her intimate knowledge of the fabric, and her expert crafting allowed the garment to fit my shape perfectly.

Ironically, the same person who could so adeptly discover the true bias of a piece of fabric was not able to detect the same quality in people, at least not in her earlier life. During each meal, from the time I was five years old and for many years following, I heard the horrific details unfold of my mother's last decade or so in Hungary and what happened to her afterward. I always wondered how my mother and her family could have missed the depth of bias that pervaded their country and even their own little world.

Simon and Hani built a house on the new part of *Fö Utca* (Main Street) in the 1930s, when all the children were adults and still living at home. A small grocery store fronted the cement build-ing, and living quarters were in the back. Full of excitement, they planted trees around and behind their new home, expecting an era of prosperity and comfort ahead.

Their exhilaration turned to grief just a few years later when Hani was diagnosed with breast cancer. Despite valiant measures to save her, including a mastectomy and recuperation in a conva-lescent home in the major city of Debrecen, she died in 1938 at the age of sixty-six. It was the eighth day of Nissan on the Hebrew calendar, just before the Jewish holiday of Passover. It turned out to be the only *Yahrzeit* (a Yiddish term for the anniversary date of a death on which mourner's prayers are recited) my mother would ever know. When speaking to me of her mother, my mothers' voice softened and shifted to one of deep reverence.

My moder, she vould vake up so early in da morning to take care her flowers, before any von else vas avake. She loved dem so much. It vas a time every day she could be by herself.

Did you help her ma? I sometimes asked, never having seen her tend flowers in my life. Even the thick-leafed pothos plant in-side our apartment was prone to dryness owing to lack of water and had lost its verdant shine in the absence of light, its leaves often turning a sickly yellow or brown.

No, I don't know anyting about taking care on flowers. I just know der names and love to look at dem.

By late 1939, my mother's oldest sister Szeren had married a widower named Herman Frankfurt and moved to Kisvarda, a larger town a few miles south of Dámóc. Dezso, who had been in exile for a while, had married and had children somewhere in Budapest, a very long way by train. Etel had recently married Szig-mund Deutsch, a widower with four young children, and moved to nearby Sátoraljaújhely. Only Laura, my mother, and their father, Simon, remained in the new home.

Living in a remote village where not many Jewish bachelors were available to marry his four daughters, Simon had difficulty in finding husbands for them. He was finally able to marry off his older two to widowers seeking wives and mothers for their children. But he still had two remaining single daughters, Laura and Sidonia, at home. They continued to help him run his grocery store and tend to his *soykher* business, bringing goods and produce to market and negotiating prices that were most advantageous to the villagers of Dámóc and the Perlstein family's cut of the profit.

With the German invasion of Poland, the year 1939 also marked the beginning of World War II in Europe. Allied countries such as Australia, Canada, France, and Great Britain had declared war on Germany, and much of the world was engulfed in mass destruction. Yet in the remote northeast region of Hungary, as my mother told the tale, the war was not something she heard about openly. In the larger cities, news traveled through whispers and rumors.

My mother remembered that in the late 1930s the Hungarian government, led by its regent, Miklos Horthy, instituted Jewish laws restricting Jewish participation in the professions and in education.

The government requested that all Jews present their birth certificates, apparently in an effort to establish their ancestry and to confirm their birthplace in order to assist in their identification as Hungarian Jews. My mother's uncle Herman from Szerencs interceded by hiring an attorney to help locate birth records, particularly for my grandfather's generation, whose documents may have been registered with local rabbis rather than with official government registries.

After their required proof of citizenship, things changed even more for the Jews of Dámóc. Simon could no longer retain a license to operate a grocery store or tavern, and it seemed that he relied solely on his *soykhering*, or trading, to sustain the family. Almost every week, my mother took what she called the little train to Sátoraljaújhely, where she carried out the family trade business and visited her sister Etel. She became friends with Etel's stepdaughter, then a teenager, who had the same first name as her stepmother. Mother and stepdaughter were henceforward known as Nagy Etu and Kis Etu, or Big Etel and Little Etel.

By 1942, the gossip in Sártoraljaújhely about the fate of the Jews in other parts of Europe grew increasingly loud. My mother's family learned that European Jews were being transported from their hometowns to forced labor camps in other regions of their home countries. Apparently, what they had heard was only a hint of the vast torture apparatus that had been implemented in countless European villages and cities and in the concentration camps of Germany and Poland.

It was impossible for the Perlstein family to imagine that such inhumane conditions really existed, or that the Nazis had a plan for the "Final Solution" for what was referred to as the Jewish Problem — total extermination. It seemed as though many of Hungary's Jews, particularly those like the Perlsteins, who lived in the countryside, were lulled into believing that perhaps they would never be deported. Even if they were, they would stand a good chance of serving only as forced laborers, returning to their homes when the war was over.

That is why, when the Nazis finally occupied Hungary in March 1944, the Perlsteins knew nothing of Adolf Eichmann or of his Kommando's plan for the annihilation of Hungarian Jews. Eichmann had waited for that assignment for quite some time, and he approached the task of deporting Hungary's more than eight hundred thousand Jews with considerable zeal. It happened quickly, starting with the eastern provinces and moving westward toward Budapest. The Jews of Dámóc, situated in the northeastern corner of the country, would be among the first wave to be cleared from their homes.

One night in late March or early April of 1944, my mother remembered the town crier banging his drum and marching through the small town, shouting *All Jews, be in front of your homes at eight o'clock tomorrow morning for departure. Bring only those things with you that you can carry.*

Here is how my mother described what occurred following the announcement:

That night, five members of my mother's family were in the house: Simon, Laura, Szeren, Dezso's eight-year-old son, little Mordcha, who had been visiting at the time, and my mother. Szeren suggested hiding their valuable jewelry, like their mother's wedding ring, gold watches, and other gold rings, brooches, and earrings, in a metal box. Looking for a secure hiding area, they all agreed that the best place would be inside the brick hearth in the kitchen. Szeren removed one brick and inserted the box in the space behind it, then replaced the brick in its original spot.

In relating this story, my mother said to me, *It made us feel good dat vhen ve return, ve gonna have dese tings vhich mean so much to us.*

They each packed a few items, including clothes, blankets, and Shabbos candles. Then, they waited, huddled close to one another, reciting the *Shema*, the most sacred of Jewish prayers, confirming the Judaic belief in one God.

The following morning, the Perlstein family came out into the street in front of their home, joining the other four Jewish families, two of them were part of the extended Perlstein family. For many years, my mother could not remember exactly who had provided the transportation for their departure. Her last memory of Dámóc occurred as she looked back at the house just one more time before leaving.

Ve left our house and ve vere already on da street vhen I turn around, and dere vas Apsi, our little dachshund. She sit so straight on da steps mit tears rolling down her face. I feel so bad dat ve have to leave her all alone, vondering who vould take care on her.

It always seemed to me that the dog was the only living creature left behind to mourn my mother and her family's exodus. Perhaps it was easier that day for her to focus on her beloved dog than on the events that tore her from the only community she had ever known. All I know is that for many years I was unable to picture the people who were the prime players in this horrible drama, but I have held a constant vision of Apsi, the weeping dog, watching her masters leave, knowing that there was nothing she could do to stop it.

9 Lining

> Unlike backing, [the] purpose [of lining] is to provide inside of garment with a finish. It often helps to preserve shape. . . Again unlike backing, which is attached and stitched with each garment section, a lining is seamed together as though it were a separate garment, and then sewn along the edges. . . . A lining covers all raw seams and edges. — "Lining," page 112

No other event since our arrival in the United States made my mother prouder than becoming a United States citizen. She had started taking citizenship classes soon after our arrival in 1949 at the Chestnut Street School, within walking distance of our North End residences on both Brookline Avenue and Osgood Street. We attended the classes together one or two nights a week for almost five years. The curriculum included instruction in civics about the Constitution of the United States and the municipal, state, and federal forms of government, as well as basic English vocabulary and phrases useful in American life.

Hanele, do you know da name of da President of da United States? My mother would drill me after class, even when I was only three years old. At first, I was too young to know the answers to her questions about politics, so I did not respond. *Harry Truman, dat's who,* she would reply, answering her own question with a smirk.

When I was older and had started to attend school, even though still very young, I began to relish the dialogue with my mother about American government and the English language. She would ask, smug in her American knowledge, *Who is da president now?*

I responded, *Dwight Eisenhower, ma, that's who,* and we would both laugh.

The classes were effective as far as instruction in civics was concerned. My mother was always interested in American rights under the U.S. Constitution and was frequently inclined to ask, even into my adulthood, *Hani, vhy can people in dis country shout der hate against Jews? Vhat vould happen if Jews shout der hate of oder people?* Even though she knew the right answer, she could never fully absorb the audacity of the Constitution. Freedom of speech was, on the one hand, something she did not quite believe possible. On the other hand, she knew it made all the difference in the world. *You know the answer to that, ma. It's right there in the Constitution.*

Despite her classroom instruction, however, she never came close to fluency in the English language. She learned to speak in her own style, not paying too much attention to word pronunciation, tense, or grammar. Sometimes she would shorten words in curious ways, such as *air condish* for "air conditioner," or *astronosh* for "astronaut," or invoke the word *gonna*, the popular contraction for "going to," (pronounced 'go-na') in the majority of her sentences.

She would often confuse me by using a masculine personal pronoun whether referring to a male or female, such as, when talking about a woman: *He came in da house.* This idiosyncratic mistake probably stemmed from the fact that her native Hungarian made no gender distinction for the personal pronouns "he" and "she." But my favorite of her grammatical transfigurations was her tendency to use the adjective "my" either in place of the pronoun "mine" or in the wrong position as an adjective. Thus, "She vas a good friend of my," or "Got my" for "my God."

Her spelling was not bad in the classroom, but out of the classroom, she spelled in a way that reflected her speech. Here is an early recipe for her pot roast gravy, which I recently found in a notebook written in her own hand: *Mix flour vith ¼ cap vater until smuth. Stir into pan juses. Bring to boiling, stiring. Reduse heat and simmer 3 minutes. Pass vith meat.*

The recipe indicates that she caught on to the odd spelling of such words as "flour, boiling, meat," and "minutes," but still insisted on inserting her own phonetic spelling for such words as "smuth, reduse, vater," and "vith." The latter word was more of a concession to proper English spelling since "th" was unattainable for her tongue. It is no wonder that her writing sample for her citizenship examination shows the following: *I go to shcoo, I go to shcool, school in this cuntry. I bay tha fod food for the home.* The citizenship officials noted that she could speak and read English but could "barely" write. She had learned and mastered enough English, however, to read her daily local newspaper from cover to cover for the rest of her days, committed to keeping up with the civic lessons she had learned in citizenship class.

Starting at age two, those citizenship classes were for me a real introduction to proper English. The foundation of my vocabulary, sentence structure, narrative ability, and love of American government started in those classes. From the time we started formally learning English and for all the years that followed, we spoke only English to each other. I heard Yiddish only in her conversations with *di grine* and sometimes in a one-way conversation with me, but she would never allow me to respond in kind.

I was exposed to Hungarian only when we visited our Hungarian cousins in New York. Otherwise, it was dropped. It sounded like a fascinating language to me, but my mother insisted, besides teaching me a few Hungarian words and phrases, such as "akarok menni NewYork ba" (I want to go to New York) and "a kis lany om" (pronounced, in my poor Hungarian, 'ah-kish-laan-yum,' my little girl), that I would be better off speaking only English. *Americans vant to speak English. Dey don't care about vhat happen to you or vhere you came from. Dey don't vant to know. You an American, you speak English,* she said many times, and I never disputed it.

Recently, I obtained our alien registration files from the Department of Homeland Security under the Freedom of Information Act, hoping to learn more about our journey toward attaining citizenship. As I read through the voluminous documents, I noted that my mother was required to have contact either by mail or in person a number of times between 1950 and 1954 with what was then called the U.S. Immigration and Naturalization Service. Not only did she provide a semiannual report as a former displaced person for both of us during her first two years in this country, but she also kept them informed annually of our address. I observed that she inadvertently neglected to file my current address along with hers on one occasion in 1952, necessitating a visit to the Post Office building, where the office was located, accompanied by her social worker from Jewish Social Services to explain the oversight.

By January 17, 1950, six months after our arrival in America, she filed her Declaration of Intention to become a United States citizen in the Commonwealth of Massachusetts, Hampden County Superior Court. I was fascinated by the photograph she had attached to the application, which was required in triplicate. Although the picture had been copied for her file, causing some blurring of her features, I could see that her hair remained in the same fashionable style of her visa photo, taken in Germany, with the same tight wave at the top, pulled back at the sides, and another wave at the bottom edge. As in that visa image, she still looks as though she is wearing no makeup but has added the now familiar red lipstick, which looks jet black in the black-and-white photo. Her face looks a little less severe than in the 1949 visa shot. As I studied this picture, which I had never seen before, I had the sense that in January 1950 my mother possessed a new sense of optimism that her life and mine might work out all right in our new country after all.

More than four years later, on August 11, 1954, after we had been in the United States for five years, my mother filed a Petition for Naturalization. She provided her physical characteristics on the application: *height, 5'5"; weight, 133 lbs; eye color, gray; date of birth, February 28, 1919; marital status, unmarried; former nationality, Hungary; occupation, machine operator.* I smiled when I noted that she had described herself, or perhaps the officials had described her, as a machine operator, which had more of an industrial ring to it than "seamstress."

As I gazed down at the section of the application that asks whether the petitioner had left the country at any time since entry to the United States, I observed a notation that we had left the country for Canada by rail for a one-week period in July 1952. Reading this entry called to mind the train trip to Montreal I had taken with my mother when I was five years old. We never spoke of this trip as I grew older, and the details remain somewhat sketchy. I recollect, however, that we visited a man and woman who had befriended my mother during their time together at the Bergen Belsen displaced persons camp, friends who had become so close that she took a week off from work, probably without pay, purchased rail tickets, and secured proper documentation to leave the country in order to visit them.

On the Result of Examination and Statement of Witnesses page, in the section under Depositions Required to Cover Residence, I read the following statement: "Sexual Act Not Adulterer, Petitioner never married." I realized, after reading this statement several times, that the immigration officials must have wanted to make certain my mother was not mistaken for someone lacking good moral character, one of the required attributes of a petitioner applying for citizenship. Along with various felonies, adultery, which may have destroyed an existing marriage, could be a ground to refuse naturalization. Her personal deposition refuting any adulterous act was duly noted.

What surprised and concurrently heartened me most as I perused all these citizenship documents was the names of those who had acted as her witnesses, who had gone to the post office with her on that Wednesday in August of 1954 to vouch for her as a candidate for citizenship. Signing their names in the Affidavit of Witnesses section are Sarah L. Greenberg, housewife, and Charles Podell, dress manufacturer, the two Americans who had given my mother a home and a job. For some reason, my mother had neglected to relate this information to me during her life, perhaps thinking that I already knew.

Reading farther down the page, I noticed something else that I had not realized or perhaps was too young to remember. It is hard to read the immigration official's handwritten scribbles in the Statement of Witnesses section following the two signatures. Written in small cursive letters in-between the lines and in the margins, as though the official were attempting to cram a great deal of data into a small space, are what appear to be the Certificate of Naturalization numbers of both Sarah Greenberg and Charles Podell, along with the dates and locations of legal citizenship. If I read these handwritten scrawls correctly, Sarah Greenberg, formerly Alpert, had earned her citizenship more than twenty years earlier, and Charles Podell more than forty years before that day in 1954.

Seeing this information for the first time helped me understand why these two people had extended their friendship to us so wholeheartedly. They must have understood the struggles and rawness of an immigrant, having experienced it themselves. They wanted to make the process easier for my mother, and perhaps for others. Acting behind the scenes, in their own way, they helped us take form and shape in a new universe.

So, on Friday, November 5, 1954, we officially became naturalized citizens. My mother swore an oath, and my citizenship automatically derived from hers. On the same day, my mother's written name was legally changed from Szidonia to Sidonia, erasing the "z" of the Hungarian spelling.

Attached to the left-hand side of the citizenship document, right above the seal of the superior court, is yet another photo, this one taken in 1954. No longer sporting the curled waves in her hair, her face, unmade except for red lipstick, looks stark and sullen. Her dark hair is pulled straight back on both the top and sides, revealing an unusually high forehead and deep-set eyes. Wearing what appears to be an inexpensive striped jersey pullover shirt with a round collar, she looks as though she has taken a hasty break from her workday in order to fit in time for the sitting. The

A portion of Sidonia's certificate of naturalization from the Commonwealth of Massachusetts, November 1954 earlier optimism is gone. She seems to be at once a working girl and a depressed woman.

10 Marking

Marking is a step a professional dressmaker never neglects but a homemaker resists. . . . Marking means transferring pattern markings to fabric sections. It is done the first thing after cutting; *do not separate* pattern pieces from sections until you have transferred marks. — "Marking," page 120

1955. The accident happened just three months after my mother earned her citizenship. Perhaps she felt that she was being a good citizen, a good American, and that I was being a good daughter. Citizenship was a turning point in our life together. Becoming a real American was the most important thing that had happened to my mother since her arrival in the United States, and, in some ways, she showed it. Despite her depressed visage, she had developed a more assured manner and concise tone, proud of her American citizen status. She was an American working woman now, pleased with her full-time job and American wages, steeped in American culture, and increasingly recognized by everyone around her for her artistic gifts and ingenuity.

Many of us *grine* kids were students at the Lubavitcher Yeshiva, our parents hoping to retain our Jewish identity lest we assimilate too quickly into a Christian America. We used to take the school bus every day from the corner of Osgood and Dwight Streets in Springfield's North End. The Sumner Avenue mansion across the street from Forest Park was occupied by the private Jewish day school. The bus rides were typical of the time: the boys pulled braids, hurled spitballs, made wisecracks, talked loudly, and the girls rolled their eyes, pretending to ignore the boys, and played cat's cradle, chatting and giggling.

Hanna, banana. Hanna, banana, some of the boys on the bus, like Simon and Joseph, shouted as they pulled my braids. In my early Springfield days, my name was pronounced with a hard "a" as in "can," rhyming perfectly with *banana*.

I pretended not to notice and continued talking with my girl-friends, who had started to giggle as they were also teased, but on the inside I was saying to myself, *Don't these boys have anything better to do than to bother me?*

We're gonna have some fun when we get off the bus. Look out for the snowballs! I heard one of the boys yell. It was the kind of February winter day children dream about. Light snow flurries had earlier added to the snow pack that was already on the ground, yet the temperature in the afternoon was slightly above freezing, so it was comfortable to be outside playing. I had already decided, though, that when I got off the bus, I would go directly home to avoid being the victim of any looming snowball attack.

It was close to 4:30 by the time our bus pulled up to the curb near our corner, still a good half hour of daylight left for outdoor activity. When the bus door swung open, I tried to be one of the first to disembark, but too many boys pushed ahead of me. Once off the bus, I looked up and quickly glimpsed the billboard of Miss Rheingold, as I always did, her smile beckoning, "My beer is Rheingold, the dry beer. Think of Rheingold whenever you buy beer." I loved looking at Miss Rheingold, the epitome of American beauty.

As I moved, my gaze passed the Esso station and looked toward our apartment building. I had taken two or three steps forward when I heard a loud, piercing scream behind me. Spinning around, I saw the bus driver, his face contorted as a tortured wail came from his mouth. In his arms was the body of a small boy, his snowsuit, hat, and crushed face covered with blood in the pattern of tire tracks, his eyes closed, and his arms hanging lifelessly by his side. I immediately recognized the child as little Benny.

I do not know why, but I must have been the first to run back to the Osgood Street apartment building to spread the news about Benny. It did not stop with telling my mother. With my adrenaline flowing, I might have been the one to tell Benny's stunned parents what had happened to their son. I kept right on going until I had told the news to everyone in the building.

What happened during that period of a few minutes is a blur, but my account must have sounded as though I had seen the accident myself. Maybe I thought I had, but the fact was that I saw only what happened in the split second after it was over. I had already started running toward the apartments when the driver was running back into the bus with Benny, some children still on the bus, clinging to their seats, and sped south toward Carew Street to Mercy Hospital. Four-year-old Benny died an hour and a half later of a fractured skull.

Nevertheless, I was identified as the key eyewitness to the accident, so when the police officers came to do their investigation, I was offered up to describe what had happened. I guess I told a convincing story because for the next several years, as the case wound its way through the legal system, I was constantly drawn out of school to go over my hapless account with attorneys and other representatives of the court. I was never sure whose side I was on or who the defendants or plaintiffs were, but I continued to tell the story I had heard from other children who *had* seen the accident.

Yes, Benny got out of the bus and went around back to

pick up some snow for a snowball, and fell. He just fell under the bus and the driver ran over him.

Did you actually see him bend down and pick up some snow? asked an attorney in a sleek gray suit.

Yes, I did.

Did you see him fall?

Yes, I did.

What happened then?

All of a sudden, he was under the bus.

And then what happened?

The driver started to pull the bus away, and then some-one screamed.

What did the bus driver do then?

He stopped and ran out to the back of the bus. He picked Benny up in his arms. Then he brought him back into the bus and drove away.

Finally, after years of telling this story countless times, an attorney crafted his line of questioning so that I blurted out the truth. I had not seen the accident at all. I had only been doing what I thought was expected of me once I was identified as an eyewitness. I was excused from the case, and it never came to the point of my testifying in court. My story may have been the truth, but I never saw it with my own eyes.

During those years, my mother and I avoided discussing the case. It was just another secret we never dared to share. That was our pattern, as sure as the markings my mother made with her marking chalk to ensure transfer of a pattern to fabric. I never revealed to her my guilt or my fear about lying. She may have thought that her daughter was doing the right thing, cooperating with the authorities. Maybe she was proud of me for being such a young witness in such an important matter. One of the children of *di grine* had died, and her daughter was a key figure in the case. She never questioned me about my involvement. She never stood up to the officials in charge to ask that her daughter not be tangled up in a legal case, nor did I ask her to relieve me of that burden.

Many years later, my mother and I attended the funeral of one of *di grine*. We were still sitting in our folding chairs at the end of the service when a short, heavy-set woman with auburn hair and melancholy eyes approached us. She looked at me and quizzically asked, *Chanele?* I stood up and nodded, *Yes.* With tears in her eyes, she hugged me very tightly and then walked away without saying another word. As I fought to collect myself, my mother leaned over and asked softly, *Hani, do you know who dat vas?*

Yes, I do, ma, I responded, almost unable to speak. *That was Benny's mother.* As I gazed back into my mother's sympathetic eyes, I felt a measure of warmth and tenderness between us — finally, a shared understanding of our feelings about a horrifying event that had happened a long time before.

11 Easing

Easing disposes of small amounts of fullness caused by a fabric edge being longer than the edge to which it is joined. . . . Easing in seams usually takes place between notches and is indicated on the pattern. . . . However, fabrics treated for easy-care and such can never be pressed entirely smooth, since they resist easing. — "Easing," page 63

The Lubavitcher Yeshiva was an impressive structure. On the outside, the white Victorian building resembled a Southern colonial mansion with four massive, two-story columns in front surrounded by double verandas with spindled railings. Inside, the large vestibule was designed in rich, dark-toned oak. It featured a grand staircase with a half turn leading to the upper floors. Dozens of children studied, played, and daydreamed in what was once the home of a wealthy nineteenth-century real estate developer. Located on Sumner Avenue in Springfield's famed Forest Park area, it was a distinct departure from my less pretentious surroundings in the North End.

Our curriculum was divided between Jewish studies, which included prayer Hebrew, Jewish laws and ritual, holidays, and Torah study, and secular subjects such as arithmetic, reading, spelling, history, and penmanship. Along with a handful of other students, I was allowed to skip kindergarten, starting the first grade at age five.

Rabbi David Edelman, the principal of the yeshiva, was a tall, slender man whose quiet mysteriousness inspired both awe and apprehension in me. I often openly gazed at him, staring while he tried to quiet noisy students in the hallways or when he prayed with his open *siddur,* the daily prayer book, in hand, his feet drawn together and his head and upper body bobbing up and down in a fluid motion.

An ardent member of the Lubavitcher Hassidic Orthodox sect of Judaism, he was always dressed in a dark suit, sometimes with the hint of *tzitzes* (the tassels on the undergarments worn by Orthodox Jews, representing God's commandments) peeking out from the bottom of his vest. A yarmulke sat on his head so naturally that it looked as though he had been born with it. When he was outside, he wore a long, dark wool coat that fell below his knees and a black fedora hat, a bountiful beard surrounding his face underneath.

The rabbi stood out among the men I had observed to that point in my young life. I sometimes imagined that I was one of his numerous children and that he was the autocratic and firm yet gentle paternal figure I yearned for, one who evoked fear and anticipation but also provided guidance and understanding.

Chana, I have a special place for you to do your drawing, I remember the rabbi saying, recognizing my fondness for doodling. *Come here to this table, and you will see the drawing paper and crayons that I have especially for you.*

Is it only for me?

Yes. I want to encourage your drawing because maybe someday, who knows, you could be an artist, he replied, revealing his teeth in a smile amid the dark mass of mustache and beard.

Thank you very much, I said, squashing my temptation to tell him how much I loved his smile, which appeared ever-more extraordinary when partially hidden by his mask of facial hair.

I progressed with my studies so rapidly that by the second grade, Rabbi Edelman phoned my mother to recommend that I enroll at Bais Jaacov, one of the orthodox schools for girls in New York City, which would mean living in New York without my mother during the school year. I never quite knew the reason for the rabbi's suggestion, whether he felt that I was, indeed, an exceptional student, one worthy of more intense Jewish learning than what was provided at the yeshiva, or whether he had concerns that I was not getting a proper example of Jewish family life from my mother. Perhaps he thought Bais Jaacov would provide me with the skills I would need to be a good Jewish wife and mother, a real *baleboste*.

Yes, Rabbi, I understand, she is very smart, I watched and heard my mother say into the phone, as I looked at her serious face. *I gonna tink about it, vhat is da best ting for Hanele,* she said slowly. *I gonna call you back to tell you my decision. Goodbye, Rabbi.* She turned toward me to tell me why the rabbi had called but did not ask whether I wanted to attend the New York school. She already knew what her answer had to be.

It might have been a selfish act when my mother declined the rabbi's offer, but I know she never regretted it. As for me, while it was true that I still possessed conflicted emotions about my mother, I did not want to leave the one human being who showed me love and affection, the one with whom I had already established a thriving sewing partnership. Even at such a young age, I already recognized my responsibility to keep up my end of the unspoken agreement I had forged with my mother to be her model. *Who else could take my place if I leave now?* I kept asking myself. I was convinced that no one could. I was content to stay with her in Springfield, Massachusetts.

The yeshiva taught me to read Hebrew prayers, to understand Jewish customs, rituals, and holidays, and to develop knowledge about the historical text of the Torah, but it did not instill a passion in me to study and pray as a method for connecting with God. At home, my mother frequently talked about her childhood experiences with Jewish observance, but she seemed to have lost much of her zeal for its practice. She gave me the impression of someone who questioned her commitment to Judaism and to a God that was supposed to help, shield, and save all who trusted in him — yet her family, which fervently adhered to its faith, was taken from her. Maybe she asked herself how she could believe in a God that had betrayed the trust of his most devoted servants. I rarely saw her in prayer or remembered her initiating any discussion about her belief in God. It was not surprising that I, in turn, possessed considerable skepticism about a personal God as I observed my mother's conflicted devotion.

If the rabbi thought I needed a more rigorous Jewish education to become an ideal Jewish wife and mother, he was right. Without the foundation of religious observance at home, a model for spiritual zeal, or the cohesiveness of a full, devout family, I had little context in everyday life for *Yiddishkeit* (Jewishness).

Perhaps it was a coincidence, but after the bus accident, many of *di grine* kids did not return to the yeshiva for the next school year but instead started public school. So, when I was eight years old and in the fourth grade, I enrolled in Lincoln Elementary School. To continue with my Jewish studies, three days a week after school I attended the Springfield Hebrew Institute next door to Beth Israel Synagogue on Chestnut Street. First, there was the transition from Brookline Avenue to Osgood Street, and then the adjustment to the Lubavitcher Yeshiva. Now I attended a public school where I needed a wooden pass for permission to take the long trek to the girls room.

Although I was younger than the rest of the students in my class, I picked up the academic studies with ease, but my shyness and sometimes brooding behavior hindered my ultimate success. My transfer to public school coincided with my developing a despondent, sullen attitude about my unclear identity, continued internal hatred for my mother, and anger at the world. My outlook seemed to emulate my mother's growing grimness and introversion during the same period. I was amazed at how one of the letters I uncovered, written in the mid 1950s, from the wife of one of my mother's cousins who had returned to Hungary after the war, seemed to corroborate my mother's attitude:

Miskolc, Hungary

My dear Szidike!

I am sorry to bother you with this letter. I remember that you did not answer our letter and there were things left between us. Believe me, oh, that there are few of us relatives, and even from so far away it would make me feel so good to keep in touch with you. On many occasions we ask Olga about you, and we always get the same answer, that you don't write her either. I imagine that you are very busy and that it's not an easy thing to work and be a student as well. I am very interested in how life is turning out for you, as at one time you were my destiny, and I can never forget you.

Feri and I speak a lot about you and especially about your beautiful daughter. I am convinced that she is a rare treasure. You sent a photo once when she was about two or three years old, and we were sure then that she was a beauty. We ask you heartily, my dear Szidike, to do for us the thing that will bring us so much joy, to write us and send us photos of both of you. As for us, thank God, we are all well. Write an answer soon.

We kiss you and with a lot of love, and your child as well.

Sevi, Feri, and the children

I instantly recognized the names mentioned in this letter from my mother's stories and from the rare opportunities I had to meet these cousins: Feri, Sevi, and Olga, my mother's surviving first cousins. After their liberation, Feri, short for Ferenc, had chosen to return to Hungary and build a family there, while his sister Olga moved to Kansas City, Missouri. Before he left to go back to his native land, however, Feri and my mother were both residents at the Bergen Belsen displaced persons camp. While there, my mother introduced Sevi and Feri to each other, which eventually culminated in their marriage, hence their "destiny."

The letter describes my mother as someone who neglected to keep in touch. She had already developed a reputation for not responding to communications from those few souls left on earth she could call her relatives. I sensed that her real mood in the mid 1950s, as evidenced by that somber photographic pose for her citizenship certificate and this letter, was one of pessimism, desolation, and uneasiness. Perhaps she felt she would be stuck with a low-paying manufacturing job for the rest of her life. Perhaps the losses of the previous decade had taken their cumulative toll or the realities of the life of a single parent in America were too tough and more so with no prospects for male companionship or marriage. Perhaps she was consumed by shame. I will never know. At the time, I did not care and never noticed my mother's depressed behavior, concerned only with my own.

Meanwhile, by the fifth grade, my conduct and the special teaching style of my teacher, Miss Beauchemin, converged into an intense conflict. She was a short, sixtyish woman whose sharp shrill voice belied her stature. She wore black orthopedic shoes.

One had an additional heel piece to prop up her shorter side. She had also a propensity to use her cane as a teaching tool. That year, I often leaned back in my chair far enough so that I lifted up the front legs to balance on its back ones.

What do you think you're doing, Miss Perlstein? Miss Beauchemin asked one day, raising one eyebrow, her cane pointing straight at my chest as though it were a sword.

Just sitting, I replied.

Well, that is not the proper way to be sitting at your desk, young lady. Put that chair down and sit up straight, she shouted, while hitting the side of my chair several times with her cane.

Okay, I will, I will, I retorted, lowering my chair but rolling my eyes back into my head, a habit that has never left me.

That's better. I don't ever want to see you doing that again. It's a sign of laziness.

I doubted, really, that it was a sign of laziness, but I did not want to get into it with Miss Beauchemin. For the second marking period, she wrote in her teacher's comments:

> *Hanna has developed a listless and indifferent attitude that has affected her work. She will be a much happier girl when she asserts herself and puts forth greater effort. She has the ability to be a more active member of the class.*

I do not know whether my mother ever read those comments, but she never chided me for my school behavior. Although my manners improved as I moved on to more empathetic teachers, I continued to have a gnawing sense of malaise, anger, and self-doubt about who I was, how I fit into my community of *di grine,* and now, into my new, broader universe. My saving graces were that I learned to ease into the world of public school and kept my feelings better hidden after the fifth grade. And, to my satisfaction, I was the best-dressed student in my school.

12 Fabrics

Making sure of fabric properties when buying has become a complex problem. A man-made fiber, simply by the process of becoming cloth, usually imitates one of the natural ones, often so successfully that we cannot tell them apart. . . . In short, it is the *label* we go by today. If it does not carry the information you want, inquire of the salesperson. — "Fabrics," page 70

1956.

Hani, Hani, come here to da vindow my. I can't believe mine eyes. I must be dreaming.

What's happening, ma? Are you okay? I answered, running toward my mother's bedroom window.

Hani, I tink a material store is moving across da street. Look, dey are taking material from da truck and bringing it into da empty building, she replied, breathless with excitement, both of us leaning out from the open window, trying to catch a better glimpse of the scene unfolding below.

Gee, ma, this is crazy. What would a material store be doing here on Osgood Street?

I don't know, but I vill soon find out! she responded, with the most joyful face I had ever seen on her.

Osgood Textile, named after the street that would hold its new fabric store, had taken possession of a vacant building directly across the street from our apartment! After their original store on

Nursery Street had burned down that summer of 1956, the owners, Herb and Lillian Kahan, lost little time in moving in the fall to their new location. My mother and I patiently waited one day before we crossed the street to enter the store. What we found was a seamstress's paradise!

Lined up on rows of long tables and shelves were thousands of bolts of closeout fabrics and remnants in many of the natural fibers my mother used for her fashions in those days: wools, cottons, and silks. It was a sea of fabric in all colors, prints, plaids, and weaves whose earthen smell filled our nostrils as soon as we walked into the one-room warehouse. While I was not a sewer, I had been around one all my life and had lived with fabrics, patterns, and threads for as long as I could remember. Watching my mother so exuberant on that first day's visit — such a departure from her previous mood — was just what I needed to boost my own frame of mind. Her newfound joy was infectious. She introduced herself to the Kahans and soon became their most prolific customer.

My mother was convinced that fate had sent a fabric outlet directly to her. She was sure it was *bashert* (destined). Since we did not own a car back then, having easy access to a source of moderately priced fabric right across the street improved the amount, type, and style of clothing we both wore henceforward. More than ever, her mind began to hold visions of completed garments. As a true right-brain thinker, she first imagined it fully in her head and then how it would look on the intended wearer, which in those days was usually me. By the time she entered the fabric store, she already knew the pattern she was seeking, the type and yardage of fabric she needed, and what lining, facing, buttons, and even thread and trimmings she would buy.

Herb and Lillian Kahan recognized my mother as a serious seamstress from the moment they met her. She came to the store often. Here is what typically happened:

Vhat do you have in a brown vool for a pair of pents for my daughter, my mother asked Herb in a very businesslike manner, her nose already leading her in the direction of the wools.

I have this remnant here I can show you, but it's less than two yards. I don't think it's enough for a pair of pants, Herb responded.

Vhat you saying? Dis is perfect, she exclaimed, often before even seeing the pattern. *It vill be enough.*

Well, I don't know, Mrs. Perlstein, I think you're going to need at least two and a half yards to fit your daughter, and I know you always like to sew in-seam side pockets.

Don't vorry about et. If you have a little rayon for da lining, I'm all set.

Herb nodded. Although he seemed doubtful, he knew she could construct the pants with less yardage than any pattern required because he understood that, to her, a pattern was just a basic blueprint. She might decide to design the pants to be more form fitting, change the width of the waistband, create a false hem, or make it longer or shorter. Her flair for creative design ensured that no garment she constructed would follow the pattern she had used exactly.

As for me, I watched with my usual combination of amazement and boredom. I respected my mother's masterful knowledge of all aspects of sewing and how self-assured she was when speaking with other sewing connoisseurs. I am not exaggerating in saying she was considered the expert in her field. But as the model and not the seamstress, I "tuned out" during our regular visits to Osgoods, since I cared little about the particulars of yardage, nap, lining, or anything else pertaining to the handicraft of sewing. They may as well have been speaking Hungarian as far as I was concerned.

The part I liked was sitting down at the pattern table with my mother and pouring over the books with her to choose the clothes she would make for me. However, since the serious seamstress had already fully envisioned the garment well beforehand, it was often an exercise in futility.

So, Hanele, vhat kind of pents vould you like?

I think I'd like some tight blue pants, ma, something that really fits snug in the rear and at the bottom.

You vant pents dat fit you tight in da tukhes and da ankles?

Yeah, I think I would look good in tight blue pants. And don't forget the pockets in the sides.

Vell, see here in Simple City [her two-word version of "Simplicity"], *dere is a paron* [pattern] *for tight pents. Da brown in da picture look so nice. I vant to see da paron so I can read da instructions.*

Ma, here's a pattern in McCall's that looks even nicer, and I think the pants are a little tighter.

Yeh, dat look nice too, but I vill read da instructions. Maybe von paron is easier to sew or has a better fit.

Yeah, maybe, but I really like this one in McCall's.

Hanele, I tink you vill really look good in da Simple City.

After reading both pattern instructions, my mother announced, *Hanele, da Simple City is da von. Let's go. Herbie, ve vill take da brown vool!* So much for my tight blue pants.

It must have been difficult for the Kahans to start over in the textile business. Osgood Street was not the best-known street in Springfield, and not all customers were willing to venture into its downtrodden neighborhood. It would take some time to build a name and attract shoppers. In the meantime, the Kahans encountered problems meeting their bottom line. A little less than a year after they opened, the Kahans asked my mother to lend them money to tide them through a difficult financial period. She was their best customer, known always to have a dollar or two saved in the bank and keenly interested in seeing their business thrive. They could not have asked a better person.

I recall Herb Kahan driving my mother to her bank to withdraw the $500 she would lend them at no interest, with only a promise to pay it back as soon as they could. There were no legal documents, no agreement in writing, not even a handshake. My mother repeated this story many times to me until she became an old woman, so proud of herself, an immigrant and a *voman alone* to be in a position to keep a business afloat.

"*I alvays have money, Hanele, alvays,* she would often say with a wry, mysterious, yet all-knowing smile, as though the knowledge of the few dollars she had saved helped to buffer our otherwise fragile economic stability. I remembered her statement when I came upon two letters that seemed to refer to another loan she had made eight years before, in Germany.

February 9, 1950

Dear Szidi!

I received your letter. It's true that it's taken two weeks to receive it since I don't live where I used to, so I'm sorry that I am answering so late. I moved because I found a job here, but unfortunately, I earn very little, a total of $20 a week, but I hope that later I will earn more. I rarely meet with my brother or other relatives. You write that I should not wait to be asked. First of all, I didn't know your address for a while,

but you can believe me that it came to my mind many times.
Once again I ask you to forgive me because I need another
two weeks or so until I can send you the money because I've
only been in America for five months and just started work-
ing. So I hope in three or four weeks to send you the money.
Once more, I apologize. I end my letter here, and I wish you
a lot of luck in your new life.

Emile

Then, a little more than two weeks later, the following letter, whose
tone and tenor had already become much less conciliatory, arrived:

February 25, 1950

Dear Szidi!
I received your letter. You really answered quickly. But one
thing surprises me. In your letter you don't mention that you
also went to the JOINT [Joint Distribution Committee],
I think, for the money, and for that other matter, and you
also gave them the names of all my relatives, however many
we have. You thought that it might help you with something,
and that there will be some harm to us. But, unfortunately,
that did not help you because neither the JOINT nor anyone
else would get involved in such a thing. I will send you the
money shortly, but now I am without work again. I end my
letter here and I remain,

Emile

These letters must have been written by the man in the story my
mother had told me only once. He had borrowed money from her

when they were both almost ready to emigrate to a new land. My mother had advised him that she would not forget the loan, and these letters confirmed her follow-up on the payback.

As I read these pieces of correspondence several times, I realized that she had written him about more than just the borrowed money. A notorious nonresponder to the written form, my mother had answered with unusual haste to the sender's letter. It must have been "that other matter" that incited her unusual interest. If she had received the information she wanted, she would not have continued to inquire.

By the time I had read these Hungarian-written letters, among the last set I had translated, I had a good idea about the nature of that other matter, and the writer's reluctance to repay his debt was unmistakable. But then there was an envelope that I found with nothing inside it postmarked June 12, 1952, stamped "REGISTERED, Return Receipt Requested," and addressed to Miss Sidonia Perlstein. The same sender's name is on the back flap. Could he have repaid the loan after all?

My mother made the brown wool pants out of the Simplicity pattern we had chosen at Osgood's. I wore it with a white, long-sleeved cotton blouse. Like all my hand-sewn garments, they fit my body as perfectly as another layer of skin and had the signature side pockets that appeared in my skirts, pants, shorts, and dresses without my asking. I miss those pockets to this day and can often be seen with my hands palpating my hips, searching for the comforting receptacle for tissues, receipts, movie tickets, keys, change, and most of all, my weary hands themselves. But side pockets usually require more fabric and labor than the typical, average-price manufacturer will invest — unlike my mother — so I live without them.

The Kahans repaid my mother's loan in full with cash and with their lifelong, devoted friendship. They went on to have a thriving fabric business, eventually moving on to bigger locations and an Internet presence, stocking millions of yards of fabric. All the while, they retained the name Osgood, the street where my mother and I lived for seven years.

13 Concealed Button Loop

An inconspicuous loop usually placed at the neck corner of an opening, often for use with a small button concealed under a collar. Use thread single; bring out at one end of loop position in a manner that will conceal knot. . . . Take three or four stitches, loose enough to form loop of desired size. Then cover with blanket stitch. — "Thread Loops," page 167

I cannot remember a time when I was not searching for clues about my father's identity. It should have been a simple act to ask my mother about him, but I was able to do it only once, when I was six years old. My mother's response was so cold and discouraging that it was enough to deter me from ever asking directly again.

On a brisk autumn day with high winds so gusty they almost blew us to the bus stop, my mother and I waited together across the street from the corner of Osgood and Main. Our hair and perfect-fitting clothes rustled in the wind, both of us staring out onto Main Street, our eyes gazing north in unison to see whether the bus to downtown Springfield was coming. It was on a purely innocent impulse that I began to ask my mother the questions she did not want to hear.

Ma, what happened to my father? I asked, never able to use the term "dad" or "daddy."

I can't talk about it, she replied, her head facing downward, not looking at me.

Why not, ma?

I can't tell you now.
When can you tell me?
I tell you vhen you sixteen.
When I'm sixteen? I repeated.
Yes. You be older den and understand better.

At that moment, the bus pulled up, and my mother and I boarded. The bus driver asked whether I was five or under because if I was, I could ride the bus at no cost. My mother opened her mouth, parting her lips horizontally in the shape of yes, but before she could utter it, I anxiously spoke up.

No, I'm six, I advised him, proud of having celebrated my birthday in the previous month.

My mother gazed down at me, gave me one of her coldest stares, and paid the driver. She was forced to pay for my bus ticket, but she had gained a ten-year reprieve from talking about my father.

Through the years, I did glean a few things about the mystery man. There was the time I had a tonsillectomy at Springfield Hospital. The admitting person asked my mother what my father's name was, and she replied, just like that: *Samuel Yungman.* So, I knew his name.

Then, there was the time when she made roast chicken with the omnipresent paprika for dinner when I was about eight, one of thousands of roast chicken meals we ate together. When I asked for the fatty piece of skin located near the chicken's rear cavity, she said, *Oh, just like der foter,* sounding like 'foo-ter' and meaning, "That's the same part of the chicken your father liked."

There was the Yom Kippur when I figured out that my father had not disappeared through death. It was the custom at our little *Russische shul* (the Russian synagogue, built by Eastern European and Russian Jews, whose foundation was laid in 1923), where most of *di grine* attended, that only those who had lost a loved one could remain in the synagogue for Yizkor, the prayers of remembrance for close relatives who have died. When the rabbi announced that Yizkor prayers would commence, all those not required to stay would rise and file out of the sanctuary. My mother always turned to me and told me to go ahead down the stairs from the women's section on the second floor and leave the building. By the time I was ten and certainly old enough to recite the Yizkor prayers with the proper seriousness, I realized that she was not asking me to leave because I was too young to participate in the solemn prayer service. It was because my father was alive.

There was that time when I was about thirteen and I had just emerged from a hot bath. With a large bath towel wrapped around my body, she wistfully observed that I was as good-looking as "der foter," again using the Yiddish word for "father" in the more formal vernacular rather than the more commonly used word "tate." As was usually the case, I said nothing when she made these side comments, but they always hit me as though someone had heaved a brick against my chest, crashing into my lungs like a steamroller. I would take a breath and say to myself, *You did have a father once, and you're a lot like him.* And that would be oddly comforting, but I still never asked, *Well, how good looking was my father, ma?*

The silence about my father led to wild fantasies about his appearance, his character, and the reasons he was not in my life. I pictured him as a tall, handsome man, always wearing a dark, fitted suit and tie, looking charming and refined. I imagined that if I knew where he lived and had the nerve to contact him, he would be so delighted at the prospect of seeing me that he would break down and cry at just the sound of my voice. He would want to see me as soon as possible. He would blame his absence on my mother, who had driven him away despite his urgent pleading, for some reason that would always remain unclear to him.

During the brief moments when my mother showed me some of her pictures taken in Germany, I noticed the image of a man whose features reminded me of my own. He fit my fantasy. He was slender and dark-haired, with naturally arched dark eyebrows and a long but well-shaped nose. His picture on a 1947 Jewish New Year card, wishing the recipient a Happy New Year in Hebrew, showed him smiling and wearing a dark suit with a white shirt and tie. I kept this image in my mind, convinced that this man was my father.

The last time my mother referred to him before I was well into adulthood, occurred when I was seventeen years old, just a couple months shy of turning eighteen. I had returned to Springfield during the summer between my first and sophomore years at the University of Massachusetts. My sixteenth birthday had come and gone without her bringing up the subject of my father as she had promised when I was six. I did not have the courage to ask, and I wondered whether she had simply forgotten the earlier conversation or just could not go through with it.

One late afternoon we were sitting in my mother's living room on her two gold-and-peach flowered upholstered chairs. She was hand sewing some skirt hems, common pins pressed into the arms of her chair as though they were oversized pincushions. I was facing away from her, sitting sideways in my chair, dangling my legs over the side, while skimming some light summer reading. Suddenly, in a husky voice and facing my back, she started to speak about one of her biggest regrets.

Maybe I should have returned to Hungary after the var, Hani. Maybe tings vould have been better.

You mean you regret coming to America, ma? I responded, never turning around for fear of breaking the unusual spell that had come over her. *I thought you liked it here.*

No, no, I don't mean dat. I love America.

Well, what do you mean then?

I mean dat if I vent back to Hungary, maybe I vouldn't meet dat jerk.

Jerk, she called him, the worst word in her language repertoire, as close to profanity as she would ever come. I immediately knew she was talking about my father.

So you really regret that, ma?

Yeh, dat vas not da kind of person I ever vanted to meet. It vas such a mistake.

Before I could ask why it was a mistake, she rose up from her chair to take a respite from her sewing in the growing darkness of sunset but unable to face me about this subject in the light. The conversation ended, and any opportunity to reopen it was dashed for years to come. Yet this short discussion was the first in which my mother expressed any feeling about my father. She was more vulnerable than I had thought. She had obviously held much inside for a long time. For the first time in my life, I sensed she was wounded by a relationship that had taken a wrong turn.

My mother and I could almost touch the air between us in the small living room that night, so dense was its presence with all that had been left unspoken. I wanted to know more about what had gone wrong in her relationship with my father. Why was she so hurt, and why did she consider it "such a mistake"? Why did she feel the need to conceal the truth? As was my pattern, I kept my mouth shut. But from that moment, I began to think just a little differently about her and my fantasy father, who was otherwise known as the "jerk."

14 Ripping out Stitching

The term seems to imply tearing apart, which is exactly what must *not* be done . . . controlled stitch-removal is easy. — "Machine Stitching," page 119

In my social work studies and in practice, I have learned that people react to terrifying, incomprehensible trauma in different ways. The most common reactions include guilt, shame, depression, anger, and most often, extreme fear. A rare few are able to tell their stories to anyone who will listen, alleviating the trauma's claim on body and soul, and most of all, on memory. Yet most survivors of trauma hesitate to share the hair-raising details with anyone except perhaps a spouse or others who have experienced similar circumstances. My mother kept her Holocaust experiences to herself for most of her life, with the lone exception of recounting as much as she could bear to me, her only close living relative.

I grew up hearing and memorizing harrowing tales of terror, brutality, loss, and courage. Starting as a five-year-old at the dinner table, I listened to idyllic accounts of life in Hungary and horrific stories of life after Hungary. The two became as routine to me as any saga a parent tells a child about the life lived before the child's existence. My mother never displayed any tears or self-pity. There were no outward signs of despair or grief, just a series of stories she unfolded a little at a time over the period of my first twenty years and then repeated over the next thirty.

I was always an intent listener to her expressive, accented voice as she described times and places, alternately torn between the enchantment of her childhood remembrances and the fear of her tales of uncategorized, indefinable madness. Sitting at a kitchen table in our small apartment in Springfield, I sensed something surreal about what she told me, something intangible about the tales that did not allow me to embrace them fully. But I usually let my mother speak for long periods without any interruption, afraid to ask anything that might stop her talking. I hesitated to jump in at the wrong time for fear that I would hurt her, or myself.

The act of recollection does not seem to recognize elapsed time, with short- and long-term memory existing alongside each other. Therefore, an event that occurred fifty years ago can often be recalled at the same time as one that happened in the past year. As such, my mother's stories were not in chronological order. Rather, she conveyed them based on whatever she had dreamed about the night before, or sometimes, as we all do, just because something popped into her head. It was not until recently that I began to gather her narratives together in my memory and think of them in sequence, like parts of a slide show. It has taken a pains-taking effort that has helped me to better understand my mother's life before I knew her and, ultimately, to better understand her actions and behavior toward me and the world.

Here is one of my mother's earliest wartime short stories, in her own words, at least as best as I can recreate it. The details still remain as clear as the first time I heard them:

> *Von day, vhen it vas almost dark, I vas in my block at Auschwitz, looking out fun da vindow, an I see a Russian voman come out of da next block mit a big turnip. She look around, and den she get down on her hands and knees, and mit her strong hands she dig a hole, so deep* [measuring perhaps six inches with her hands] *in da ground, and she put*

in da turnip. Den she put dirt over it. I know on dis second,
I vill go out vhen da sun go down and take a chance, before
da guards see me, to dig up dis turnip and bring it back to
my block. So I did it, and Laurie an me an some of da oders,
ve eat it just like dat. Ve don't even tink about it.

As a child, this story roused my imagination about my mother's daring prowess, her courage in the face of stacked odds, and her ability to exhibit prodigious physical and emotional strength. It showed me that she placed such a high value on survival that she was willing to risk her own capture for it. I was able to listen over and over again to this story without ever feeling bored, but more than that, it made me feel secure to be in my mother's care.

Just a few hours after leaving Dámóc, my mother and her family arrived in the nearby city of Sátoraljaújhely, where the Nazis had established a ghetto to concentrate the Jews they had rounded up from the surrounding northeastern villages. Now when I read accounts of the Nazi sweep of Hungary, I realize that the few Jews of my mother's town were among the first to be taken under the orders of Adolf Eichmann as part of "Operation Margarethe." This was the Nazi occupation of Hungary, which began on March 19, 1944, and was perhaps the most organized and controlled such operation ever completed.

Ve all go to my sister Etel's apartment in Sátoraljaújhely.
Maybe tirty or forty people stay in her tree rooms. Me shrayt
un vaynt [people screamed and cried], *vorried vhat vould*
happen to dem because, believe me, ve really don't know.

Their arrival at the ghetto happened to coincide with the Jewish holiday of Passover, when Jews all over the world celebrate their ancestors' exodus from the land of Egypt after centuries of bondage.

Despite their condition as captives, the Jews in Sátoraljaújhely had every intention of observing the Passover holiday. Yet inherent in this observance was the adherence to the dietary laws required during Passover's eight days, commemorating the haste of the Jewish people as they left to dwell in the wilderness without sufficient time to allow their bread to rise. Although matzo, the unleavened bread symbolic of the freedom and humility of the Jews after they departed Egypt, had been prepared in their home village of Dámóc before their expulsion, the Perlsteins were unsure how they would obtain traditional food in the ghetto.

Their Passover concerns were assuaged by my great-uncle *Shayme,* who was one of the wealthier residents of Dámóc and who had connections with the Hungarian police stationed in the ghetto. Shayme arranged, with the aid of a sympathetic Hungarian police officer, to retrieve supplies from Shayme's home in Dámóc for Passover. Thus, food such as matzo, kosher wine, apples, and nuts were brought to the cramped quarters where my mother was staying. It is uncertain whether they arrived in Sátoraljaújhely before the start of Passover, which would have been on the evening of April 7 of that year, or sometime between then and the last day of the holiday, April 15. But as my mother told the story, she was able to celebrate the Passover of 1944 among the crying souls of my aunt's apartment. They had, after all, amid the chaos and agony around them, obtained their holiday food.

By the middle of May 1944, the Hungarian gendarmes began to round up the Jews in the Sátoraljaújhely ghetto for deportation.

Ve all came out of da building mit our suitcases. My sister Szeren vas valking ahead of us, alvays so strong. Da police shout and push us to da train station. Vhen ve came to da station, ve look up to see a line of cattle cars vaiting for us. Ve vondering vhere ve are going, scared of not knowing. But ve are still tinking dat ve go to a vork camp somevhere in Hungary.

She could always tell by the focused look on my face, even when I said nothing, that I wanted to hear more. It was a scene that took place countless times during my childhood — my mother recounting her stories and me rapt with attention, as though I were hearing an author read chapters from her book. Once she began a narrative, she continued without hesitation until the end.

Ve climb into da train mit maybe a hundert oder people in our vagon. Vhen dey close da door, I could hear da bar click outside an den gants geshlosn [completely locked]. *Da lock sound seem so loud to me as if da eart was shaking.*

Then she went on to describe the conditions in the cattle car on the three- or four-day trip to Auschwitz in Poland. There was not enough room for everyone to sit down on the floor, so my mother and her sisters stood up during most of the grueling trip, allowing my grandfather, already seventy-five years old, and their nephew, little Mordcha, to sit down. With no food or sanitary facilities, my mother felt faint, nauseous, and hallucinatory most of the way, while many of those in the same wagon were either unconscious or had died during the journey. Soon she encountered the first hint that they had left Hungary.

Von night, vhen it vas raining, I put out my hand from da small vindow opening to try to catch some raindrops on my finger. Vhen da train pass by a station, I strain to see da name. It say "Krakov." In dat moment, I knew ve vere not going to a vork camp in Hungary. Ve vere so wrong hoping ve could stay near our home. Ve vere in Poland, and vhen

*I turn to tell Szeren vhat I see, she look at me and say dat
our life in Got's hant now.*

A short time after seeing the sign for Krakow, my mother and her
family arrived at Auschwitz. A recently constructed railroad spur
led them directly inside the Birkenau camp, a sprawling area of
wooden barracks, gas chambers, crematoria, and watchtowers.
The bar on the door of the cattle car was lifted, the door opened,
and those who were still alive in my mother's wagon were herded
out by men in striped prison uniforms who shouted at them to
leave their belongings in the cattle car, that they would be brought
to them later. Within a few moments, they were grouped into
selection lines. Here is what happened in the span of just a few
minutes:

As they were separated into lines of men and women, five in
each row, my mother's oldest sisters, Szeren and Etel, each held little
Mordcha's hands, trying to comfort and protect him. My mother
and Laura walked hand in hand beside them. As dogs barked, S.S.
officers shouted, *Men to da left and voman to da right.* My grandfather Simon was pushed into the men's line, as were some of the
male cousins and extended family who had been with him and my
mother's family in the ghetto. When the women came to the head
of the line, they were greeted by a smiling, young, dark-haired man
in a sparkling clean, starched uniform decorated with an iron cross
medal. He appeared to be waving a riding crop, indicating either
the right or left. The group's innocence regarding its fate, even on
the precipice of death, seemed to have been a source of mockery
for the man. As they approached:

*Laurie ask him, 'Vhat is dat dark smoke and strong
smell?' He tell her in perfect Hungarian, 'Dat is your moder.'
She look at him not understanding vhat he mean because*

our moder vas already dead for six years. Den he look at us up and down vhile ve vere still dressed in da clothes ve had been vearing for many days, and he point to da left for Szeren, Etel, and Mordcha, and to da right for Laurie and me. Ve never see vhat happen to my fader. Ve vere all crying, but it happen so fast, ve couldn't say goodbye. Ve never saw any of dem again.

Soon, my mother and Laura were taken to an area where they were stripped of their clothes, bathed, deloused, shaved, and supplied plain sack dresses, tied at the waist, as well as prisoner numbers. As a child, I had seen many tattooed forearms among *di grine*, with distinct blue concentration camp prisoner numbers. But unlike the million souls who came before them, my mother and her sister never had their prisoner numbers burned onto their skin. The frantic pace of registration for the Hungarian Jews who arrived at Auschwitz with such speed and frequency meant that a few thousand of them were assigned serial numbers but not tattooed. It did not matter. The numbers were seared into my mother's brain, and she retained them in her memory for the rest of her life.

I discovered those infamous five digits in the early 1980s when my mother and I visited a bank in Springfield. As we completed the application for a new account, the teller asked whether we wanted ATM cards. My mother had never owned an ATM card before, so the teller explained that we would have private, secure personal identification numbers, which we could use to perform bank transactions at its ATM machine. I took my mother aside.

Ma, do you have any favorite numbers you want to use? I asked. *They have to be ones that you'll remember. We can each have our own set.*

I have a number dat I remember from a long time ago,

and I have von for you too, she replied without any reflection.

Okay. What are they?

Mine is eleven tousand, von hundert un five, an yours is eleven tousand, von hundert un six.

Where in heck did you get those? I asked, flabbergasted.

Dat vas mine an Laurie's concentration camp numbers.

Without asking any further, I keyed in 1-1-1-0-5 and 1-1-1-0-6.

15 Style

> Patterns are offered in a wide variety of *styles,* . . . *figure-types,* and in just about as many *sizes* as women and girls come in. Which combination of these is right for you, or how to alter the nearest fit to your figure, is what concerns us here. *Style* is design and has nothing to do with fit. . . . Here there is no trying on before buying! — "Patterns," pages 127 and 128

By 1959, many of *di grine* left Springfield's North End in favor of the Forest Park section of the city, including us. Most of them had moved up in the world since their arrival as immigrants a decade before. They had learned to compete effectively in America's economic life, buy businesses, save and invest their money, and improve their command of the English language. Many were able to buy their own homes or rent nicer quarters in a more attractive part of the city. That summer, when I was twelve years old, I went to visit my mother's cousin Olga and her family in Kansas City, my first venture away from home on my own. During the time I was gone, my mother prepared for our move to an upstairs six-room apartment on Maryland Street near the former zoo entrance to Forest Park.

Lazar and Beatrice Stambovsky, good friends of the Kahans of Osgood Textile, owned the 1920s two-family house. Consisting of well-kept yet modest two-family houses on small plots, the working-class neighborhood included residents of various ethnicities, including Italian, Irish, and Jewish. The Forest Park homes allowed *di grine* to remain close to one another, but no longer in the intimate setting of the block on Osgood Street.

We turned one of our new three bedrooms into a sewing room and split up my mother's bedroom set for the two remaining bedrooms. She took the bureau with the large mirror and one nightstand, and I took the dresser and the other nightstand. The bedrooms, unlike those on Osgood Street, were so small that they offered scant walking space. But compared with the previous apartment, where I had only a donated Hollywood bed and cardboard boxes for furniture, it was a step up. I remember the thrill I felt when I opened and shut the dresser drawers over and over again to check out my folded clothes, costume jewelry, and anything else I pleased.

That next year, 1960, was in many ways a watershed year for my mother and me. Over the previous two years, until the spring of 1960, when I was almost thirteen, I had grown from five feet one inch to five feet eight inches tall. In those days, that was very tall for a girl just reaching puberty. My burgeoning hormones also saw the development of small round breasts, a narrow waistline, and shapely hips. My most noticeable physical attributes, however, were my long and lean legs, the source of teasing from my fellow classmates at Forest Park Junior High School.

Hey, Hanna the banana, how does it feel up there? yelled some of the boys during recess, reprising that old *Hanna, banana* verse. *Banana Peelstein, are you up on stilts or what?*

As usual, I pretended not to notice the taunts, sometimes throwing posture to the wind and leaning forward, as though I had a crick in my back, in an effort to appear shorter. If I could just reduce my height, I thought, I would appear more attractive to those sarcastic boys in my class, who were almost all of diminutive size compared with my long, skinny frame.

Hani, how many times I have to tell you to stand up straight?

continued my mother's never-ending refrain while she was fitting a three-quarters-finished skirt. *Pick up your chin and push your shoulders back,* she reprimanded. *You a tall girl. Stand up like a model. Ve gonna make da most special clothes for you now.*

Aw, ma, I moaned, *I'm sick of standing up for so long. Anyway, it hurts my back to stay in the same position. Why do you always make me put on shoes and wear a girdle when you're fitting? How much longer is this going to take?* She clenched her teeth and made an exasperated noise from inside her throat. *You making dis very hard for me, Hanele. You really making dis very hard.*

In that spring of 1960, we attended Simon Fuchs's bar mitzvah, one of *di grine's* highlight events of the year, to which everyone in the community was invited. The Fuchs family was popular among *di grine,* congenial with just about everyone.

Simon and I had known each other since we were four years old. We had discovered each other's anatomies by the light of a Howdy Doody lamp when we were five and living on Osgood Street, attended the Lubavitcher Yeshiva together, witnessed the same bus accident, vacationed together at resorts in Moodus, Connecticut, in the late 1950s, and often sat on a couch in his living room and talked and laughed.

My mother and I looked forward to Simon's bar mitzvah, since by the end of the 1950s, our isolation resulted in few invitations to social occasions. Her imagination about what kind of dresses we would wear began whirring well before the event. From a photo of her at the bar mitzvah, I notice that by 1960 her hair was cut in a short perm, her lips sported the now-familiar dark-red lipstick but no additional makeup. She was wearing a short-sleeved, scoop neck, light solid-colored cotton dress on her then-lean frame, a distinctly plain and unassuming outfit compared with the dresses of the other women, who were *oysgeputst,* gussied up, in their finest party clothes.

For me, she had outdone herself. Made of white raw silk, my dress possessed some of the style attributes that would mark her later fashions. A single strand of fake pearls peered out from the simple neckline, which was cut in the shallow curve of a bateau shape. The short sleeves of the dress were puffed into a bouffant, cinched with elastic at the bottom. Gathered at the waistline, it flowed into a very full skirt enhanced by a soft petticoat and offset by a thin gold belt. It had simple features, no ruffles or extra adornments, and yet it drew the attention of everyone in the room. *Hanele, du bist azoy sheyn!* [you are so beautiful!]. *An vhat a dress!*

Keynehore, many of the women said that night, followed by spitting three times, a ritual I knew, having witnessed it before, though I never fully understood its meaning. Usually pronounced 'caan-ne-hor-eh' among this group of Yiddish speakers, *keynehore* means 'no evil eye' and is a word I always took to be some sort of compliment. It was not that at all.

I had already achieved my full height by that time, which helped to show off the youthful elegance of the dress and the talent of the person who had made it. The occasion marked the first time I can remember that my mother observed, upon our return home, *Hani, you vere da best-looking von tonight. Dat dress fit you like a qveen.* Those words, "fit you like a qveen," resonated in my head like the thrill of finally

At almost thirteen years old, the author, wearing Sidonia's creation, a raw silk white dress passing an audition after many futile attempts. I felt enormously proud that I had earned that special accolade from her. Yet I remember having the most profound headache that night, causing me to take to my bed.

Vhat's a matta, Hanele? my mother asked me with a concerned look.

I have a pounding headache, ma. I'm not sure why.

I know vhy, she remarked. *Dose people, dey give you a nehore. I'm sure.*

Amid the pain and fogginess of my headache, I began to realize the true meaning of keynehore. When my mother said the word, separating out its last three syllables, ne-ho-re, I sensed that she was referring to a ruthless curse that had befallen me.

It was not until I reached adulthood that I learned about the centuries-old Jewish belief in invisible demons that lived purely to squash a person's hopes and dreams and thwart her happiness. When *di grine* admired my looks and dress, they followed those expressions of delight with keynehore and the spits to shoo away the demons that might burst my balloon of contentment. But perhaps someone had omitted the supplemental gesture in her admiration, casting a nehore my way. Even though I never believed in curses, or rather, ever really thought much about them, I nonetheless nodded and said, *Yeah, maybe that was it.*

My growth spurt happened to coincide with John F. Kennedy's presidential campaign and eventual victory in November of 1960. My mother and I were fascinated by the charm and electricity that John Fitzgerald Kennedy, our home-state senator, exhibited on the campaign trail and his appeal to working-class families. We were even more captivated by his fashionable wife, Jacqueline. Her image appeared on the cover of every popular magazine, newspaper, and television news show. What caught our eye, from the moment of her husband's inauguration, was the sheer simplicity and elegance of her designer clothes, from casual leisure outfits to stately suits and gowns. My mother was enthralled from the moment she saw Jacqueline Kennedy, and that enchantment lasted throughout the next several decades, manifesting itself in countless items in my wardrobe, transforming it from fashionable to couture.

In 1960, my mother was promoted at the Victoria Dress Corporation from sewing machine operator to forewoman. She had worked there for more than nine years as one of the best machine operators ever to grace a dress manufacturer's door. Mr. Podell judged her ready to join management, and indeed, she was a good sewing teacher and supervisor to those who really wanted to learn the art, although I never joined that group. In the next few years, she had the opportunity to meet the very young and dashing Edward Kennedy on his first campaign tour for senator from Massachusetts. *Hani, he came in to da shop an shake my hand, just like I shaking yours now.*

She was given two free tickets to see *My Fair Lady* on Broadway and a night at a New York City hotel, a bonus from a contractor in New York's garment district. It does not mean we did not have a good time — just because we left the show after the first act, thinking it was over, neither one of us having been to a theater performance before. Luckily, many of the best songs were in the first act, and I sang "I Could Have Danced All Night" until we returned to Springfield the following day. My mother took great delight in seeing me so happy, and for one of the few times in my life, she displayed a relaxed smile.

Her new responsibility as forewoman and the additional income it brought enhanced my mother's self-esteem. She was visibly more secure in her life situation, purchasing our first car, a 1961 beige Chevy Impala with a white stripe on the side, the envy of many of our neighbors. But still far from living in style, we spent much of the increased paycheck on sewing patterns, fabric, notions, and accessories for my wardrobe.

Just before my move to Forest Park, however, when I was eleven, I had fortuitously learned about the shocking details of menstruation. I was walking home one day from the Springfield Hebrew Institute, my after-school religious academy, when Pearl Smolarz, one of the children of our immigrant community and three years my senior, divulged the graphic details of a woman's biological fate. After Pearl's revelations, I walked the rest of the way home thinking that this was just one more secret my mother had kept from me. When it happened to me that year, in 1960, I was prepared for it without ever having asked my mother for an explanation, relieving her of the dreaded task.

On one hand, I was pleased that my mother now found me so ideal for exhibiting her exquisite design creations, so much more sophisticated now. On the other hand, I was appalled at my sudden conversion from little girl to young woman. My body belied my inner insecurity. I had to stand up straight at home but turned into a hunchback during the school day. At the same time, my wardrobe developed a duality marked by high-fashion clothes for nonschool events and switched to homemade skirts and blouses for school.

We graduated from Simplicity and McCall's patterns to Vogue and Butterick. Like "Jackie" Kennedy, my mother was fond of straight, sleek skirts or slight A-line sheath dresses and tailored jackets and suits, simple cuts with no frills. At the same time, button selection began to assume one of the most important aspects of her creative process, often delaying the completion of a garment, like a blazer jacket, owing to the time required to find just the right set of buttons. Incredibly, they often matched the color and design of the fabric and trim. Sometimes, to the uneducated eye, they seemed not to match at all, but when applied to the outfit, were just the perfect finishing touch.

Starting in the 1960s, the clothes my mother crafted reflected a woman with a keen sense of modernity and style. Her creations seemed inconsistent with someone who had grown up in a small agricultural European village, far from the urbane centers of culture and sartorial splendor. To add to the contradiction, the Victoria Dress Corporation produced everyday dresses with little sophistication or design style. Thus she had her daytime obligation to mundane fashion and her off-hours propensity for couture. We both seem to have led double lives in the early 1960s.

16 Patterns

If after buying a pattern and comparing all its actual measurements with your own, you discover that another figure-type or size would require less alteration, we suggest that you buy this other pattern. — "Patterns," page 129

1965. The side door to the house leading to the creaky, dark back stairway was open. I climbed the winding stairs to find the door to our second floor apartment ajar. As I entered through the kitchen, I heard muffled sobs coming from my mother's bedroom. I tiptoed toward the room and stopped at the entrance. It was not our habit ever to close bedroom doors, so when I peered in, I saw my mother lying supine on her bed, fully clothed, including shoes and jacket, as though she were ready to go to work. Her left arm was raised above the back of her head on the pillow, while her right hand was covering her eyes as though sheltering them from the light. The sound of her cries was so foreign to me that I moved closer to better determine its source. At that moment, she removed her hand from her eyes and looked up at me, saying in a low voice, *Hani, mine life is over.*

A few days before this scene, I had called home from the University of Massachusetts at Amherst, where I was a seventeen-year-old first-year college student, having graduated from Classical High School when I was just sixteen. Reversing the charges as usual on the payphone in my dorm, the monotone voice on the other end was alarming.

Hi, Hani, how you?

I'm okay, ma, what's new with you?

I okay, too. But I tink maybe dere gonna be changes at da shop.

What changes at the shop, ma?

Mr. Podell, he speak to me about leaving da business.

What does that mean for you, ma?

I don't know, Hani, I don't know . . . Her voice drifted away.

I'm worried about you, ma. Your voice sounds weird to me.

Don't vorry. I gonna be fine.

Her distant voice over the phone concerned me. I could tell that the changes occurring at the Victoria Dress Corporation, which she described so laconically, were having more of an effect on her than she conveyed on the phone, so I asked a fellow student to drive me from Amherst to Springfield one mid week morning. As I looked at her now, lying on the bed, her tear-soaked face and shaking voice betrayed her true condition, which had been presaged by that phone call. I pressed her to tell me what was really happening, and with a mixture of reluctance and relief, she finally revealed the events of the previous few weeks.

Mr. Podell had decided to retire and sell the Victoria Dress Corporation, she told me. Johnny, the foreman, seized the opportunity to buy the business and promptly told my mother that he would not retain her services as forewoman. She could stay if she wished, he offered, but only as a sewing machine operator.

My mother's pride prevented her from accepting Johnny's offer. She was willing to be a machine operator again, but not at the Victoria Dress Corporation, where her demotion would be in plain view for all the other employees to see and become food for their gossip. Without my knowing it, she had tried her hand at operating sewing machines at some factories in nearby Chicopee, but she found it difficult to accustom herself to a new company.

For the first time in my life, my mother seemed defeated. She had survived horrible adversity and had successfully made a life for us both in the United States. Now, circumstances had reversed her fortune again. I found myself assuming a motherly role, trying to console her, boosting her confidence, even though I had no idea how she would get her career back on track.

> *It's going to be okay, ma. You'll see. You're the best sewer in the world.*
>
> *No, Hani. I don't know vhat to do. Sewing da only ting I know, but dere is no vork for me. Vhat's gonna happen to us?* she lamented, as she turned her head from side to side.
>
> *Maybe there's a different way for you to use your sewing talent, ma. Maybe you won't have to work in a factory. Maybe people could pay you for sewing,* I suggested, as I moved my position to different sides of her bed in an attempt to talk directly to her face.
>
> *No, I never make enough money to live. Nobody know how I sew.*
>
> *You could ask around and see if there are some people who need a seamstress and try to make a go of it,* I suggested, but I really had no idea what I was talking about.

She stopped her tossing for a few moments as though my recommendation had caused her brain to compute an account balance sheet in just a few seconds and said, *Tank you, Hani. I gonna tink about it.* Then she added, *Oy, vos fur an eytse,* as though mumbling to herself. I did not know exactly what this often-used Yiddish statement of hers meant, but the inference was something like,

"Oh, what kind of mess am I in?" or "What kind of advice should I take now?"

At my mother's urging, I left her lying on the bed and returned to the University of Massachusetts, not knowing what would become of her or her ability to make a living for us. To be honest, once I got back to the campus, I did not think much more about her. I was content to be away from home and from my mother, away from endless fittings and pattern searches, and away from the constant pressure to meet her academic and fashion expectations. College was a breather from my mixed emotions about a mother who was suffocated by unrelenting pride and unable to share the truths of my identity.

By then, I had grown more comfortable with my body and height. I had taken to calling myself by my given name, the one that had been my grandmother's, pronouncing the first "a" in "Hanna" with a more gentle sound, such as in "Hanukkah." Although still somewhat of a loner, I became so immersed in campus social life and my exams that I blocked out the soul searching that consumed my mother.

When I returned home after spring break, just a few weeks later, she had undergone a complete transformation. Gone were the tears of desperation and disconsolation. In their place, my mother had a renewed spirit of optimism and aspirations for the future. She had made some contacts and found a handful of customers who were interested in having a personal seamstress, women who, for the most part, were the wives of professional men and could afford the expense of handmade clothes and alterations. One of *di grine*, Mania Lasker, had given her a Pfaff sewing machine converted from manual to electric to replace the malfunctioning Köhler she had brought from Germany. She used the Pfaff for the rest of her life but always kept the Köhler in her sewing room.

See, Hani, I have dese cards, she beamed, showing me her new, plain-white business cards, which read "Sidonia Perlstein, Dressmaking and Alterations."

So you think being your own boss will work, ma?

Yeh, I gonna try. If dese customers tell oder people, maybe I can have enough business to make a living.

I'm glad to see you're happier, anyway, I said, and I really meant it.

As the weeks and months continued, my mother's sphere of customers grew steadily, and by the end of the decade, she had acquired many who brought thoughtful ideas for new creations and requests for alterations. She began to work all hours of the day and night to meet the demand for her services, but she seemed to love every minute of it. As her home business grew, she earned enough money to continue supporting us, perhaps even more than her earnings at the Victoria Dress Corporation, although the exact amount was known only to her.

I grew fonder of the new Sidonia Perlstein who had become more comfortable with human interaction, particularly with her customers, than she had been as a factory worker. These *Americanishe* (born in America or Americanized) women seemed to bring out a sense of humor and self-confidence in her that had remained hidden when I was a child. Her expressiveness and animation when talking about these new people in her life, their families, and their unique sewing requests brought her formerly taciturn manner to life.

Even though she remained restrained toward me in her praise of anything I may have accomplished, her verbal admiration usually reserved for my appearance in her beautifully designed clothes, she apparently gushed about her wonderful daughter to any and all who would listen. I understood this from having met her many customers on the street or in stores, all of them acknowledging me without any introduction. It was through the laudatory words of these customers that I learned how I was doing in my mother's eyes. Looking back, I often wonder whether her reticence in praising me was a result of her caution about risking the nehore she had first mentioned to me when I was twelve, the evil eye that would quash my dreams or spoil my happiness.

During this time, my mother further developed her enthusiasm for couture fashion and imaginative design, which benefited me as much as it did those for whom she sewed. The fabrics and styles she used for these new individuals in her life were frequently transferred to my wardrobe. A few fabric remnants from a wool crepe pantsuit made for a customer, for example, may have been transformed into a wool crepe vest and very short miniskirt in my clothes closet. Osgoods remained the outlet for many of the patterns and fabrics my mother used to sew her customers' clothes. Often, they would trust her to make the purchase after explaining what they had in mind. At other times, my mother traveled with them to Osgoods to assist in making the choice.

It was an era that ushered in a pattern of continuous measurement. She filled countless notebooks with the body dimensions, written in Hungarian, of everyone for whom she sewed, and none was taken more often than my own. It's not an exaggeration to say that my mother took my measurements more than twenty times a year until her age and physical decline prevented it. The frequency did not change much when I stopped growing and my body remained the same for a long time.

I cannot say that I minded her constant need for measurements. It helped me to keep tabs on my own body shape, since I was careful to watch my diet to ensure minimal changes in my weight, knowing that she would notice even the slightest fluctuation in my dimensions. I knew that she was concerned that a slight weight loss or gain, different shoes, style changes, menstrual cycle, posture, pregnancy, and any other factor would throw off her meticulous calculations for size and fit. The points she most often measured were bust, waist, hips, sleeve length, back and front shoulder to waist lengths, inseam, and the all-important number of inches from the floor for a skirt hem. It was this last measurement that varied the most, ranging from nineteen to thirty inches at various stages.

Tirty inches from da floor! I don't believe it, Hani. I don't do tirty inches for anyvon but you. Vhat a short skirt you vearing, my mother exclaimed at a measurement taken during one of her visits in my junior year at UMass. She pretended to be dismayed at the shortness of the magenta corduroy skirt that seemed even shorter when I wore my three-and-a-half inch high heels, zooming me to almost six feet tall. As we ate the chicken *paprikash* my mother had prepared, my roommate, Janice, and I wondered whether it were truly possible that she had never gone any shorter.

I can go longer if you want, ma. Do you want to go down an inch? I teased.

No, dat's okay, Hani. Dat look good to me, she marveled. I knew it was just the way she wanted it.

In my senior year, I was nominated for the Best Dressed Co-ed on Campus and modeled three of my mother's handmade designs in the final contest: a casual, short, brown wool-tweed A-line skirt with a cream-colored turtleneck sweater, a wool-silk blend fuchsia designer suit, and a hot pink silk satin long gown. As I walked across the stage in the Student Union ballroom showcasing each of these outfits, I checked where my mother was sitting, stopped in front of that part of the audience to look straight at her, turned around, and walked backstage, never before so proud of her.

I realized that I wanted to win that contest not so much for me as for her, to acknowledge her great artistic gifts publicly. In the end, someone else won, but it was enough for me to compete and model some of her lovely handmade designs before hundreds of people. After the event, she was her usual closed-mouthed self, but the softness in her eyes told me she was pleased. When I arrived home for my last visit before graduation, she pointed to her cutting table.

Look, Hani, von of my customers give me a sewing book. It's my first von.

Do you think it will help you to sew better, ma? I joked, picking up the large orange book featuring a rose-pink spool of thread, a sewing needle, and a four-holed button on the front cover, and two pattern pieces and a tracing wheel on the back.

No, but I like et here in my sewing room. It show I am a serious sewer, she responded, as though not aware that the world already knew.

I glanced at the book's title, *Coats and Clark's Sewing Book: Newest Methods from A to Z,* destined to be the only sewing book she would ever own, and laid it back on her table.

17 Clipping

A clip is a straight cut through seam allowance to within a thread of the stitching line. Clip once into a corner; clip enough times around a curve to make it lie flat. The more pronounced the curve and the firmer the fabric, the more clips are needed.
— "Facings," page 83

My mother's stories grew more terrifying as I grew older. They became so intense that when she spoke of them, I would hold my breath at regular intervals during her narrative until I felt light-headed and nauseous. I thought, at any moment, my mother would notice my queasiness, but she was always so engrossed in her storytelling that she never observed it, or at least she never mentioned it. So, I never asked her to stop. There we were, always only the two of us, seated at the kitchen table, the storyteller and the devoted, enraptured listener, spellbound by tales that a child should never have had to hear.

On their first day in the camp, my mother and her sister Laura and some of their cousins were chosen to be slave laborers, destined to survive another day. They soon understood that the source of the dark, dense smoke and pervasive, putrid smell they sensed upon their arrival at the Birkenau camp came from the chimneys of the crematoria used to burn the bodies of those who had been killed in the adjoining gas chambers — including their sisters Etel and Szeren, their eight-year-old nephew, Mordcha, and their father, Simon.

It did not take them long to notice that there were few children in the camp. When they asked their fellow prisoners about it, they were told that most children were immediately gassed along with their mothers or other caretakers. If either my mother or Laura had been holding little Mordcha's hand instead of Etel and Szeren, it would have been she who was sent to the gas chamber along with him.

Roll calls — countless, everlasting, soul-sucking roll calls — marked their time at Auschwitz. As they settled into the prison routine, they often awoke before dawn and were hustled into rows of five to line up for the morning roll call, referred to as the *appel*. At times, they were left standing at attention at arm's length from one another for hours on end in the hot summer sun, observing other prisoners fall dead from total exhaustion, or if not yet dead, then shot as they were about to hit the ground. As new arrivals, they discerned that many of the prisoners around them had already been at the camp for many months, even years. My mother described one vision in particular that led me to a rapid understanding of their dire circumstances:

> *Hani, ve look around an see dat ve are surrounded by barbed vire. Ve vere vatching people just touch da vires and dey vere dead right avay. At first, ve couldn't understand vhy dey run into da vires vhen dey know dey vill die. But later ve knew. Dey give up hope.*

Laura and my mother were assigned to the *Scheisskommando*, the work team in charge of cleaning latrines. Although I have since seen photographs of concrete latrines in designated blocks at Birkenau, as I remember my mother's description, the latrines were constructed in the open air, exposed to the elements, and covered on top with long planks of wood punched with holes on which prisoners sat, if they could make it in time, to defecate.

> *Von time, Laurie and me vere bending down to dig out da mess from da latrines vhen ve hear a loud laugh above us. Ve look up to see da same man who meet us at da train platform. By dat time, ve knew he vas Dr. Mengele, who vas known for his brutality. He vas smiling down on us and say to us in Hungarian, 'Did you ever tink in your life dat you two vould be doing dis?' I can never forget his evil face and his perfect, neat uniform, looking down on us an making fun of us. He vas taking pleasure from our misery.*

But aside from Dr. Mengele's mockery, the assignment seemed to shelter the two somewhat from attracting the attention of the S.S. guards. The rotten stench from the latrines, and their feces-stained clothes and bodies helped to keep the guards from harassing or beating them. The women who made up the crap squad, as I later called it in my own mind (not in the spirit of ridicule but to ease my intense fear), were able to talk and interact with little interruption from their overseers.

Ve sometimes even come togeder an sing Shabbos songs, just like ve used to sing at home, she remarked, remembering when the women of the Scheisskommando, and sometimes other prisoners using the latrines, fluently sang the tunes they had sung every Shabbos in their homelands.

It has always been inconceivable to me that my mother could tolerate the absence of human norms regarding bodily cleanliness and the handling of human excrement. Yet I learned that when fighting for her own and her sister's survival, she was capable of almost anything. On one occasion, someone from the men's camp at

Auschwitz told them across the barbed wire that he had once seen their brother, Dezso, who had departed Hungary from a different location. Later, Dezso vanished and never appeared again.

Ve vere so happy to hear Dezso vas alive, even if dey just see him von time. He vasn't selected for da gas chamber. Dat mean maybe he had a chance to live and survive. But they would never know whether he had survived Auschwitz, was transported to another camp, lost his life to starvation or disease, or died by other murderous means. My mother never heard of him again.

The two sisters endured numerous "selections" that occurred routinely. The camp doctors and members of the S.S. made them strip naked and run past them to see whether they were still fit for manual labor. My mother's varicose veins ("varical" veins, as she called them) were always a source of trepidation at the time of selection. Each time, Laura would say, *If you run fast, Szidike, maybe dey don't see your legs.* On another occasion, my mother heard someone in the prisoner group saying, *If dey see dose veins, you gonna die.* Somehow, both my mother and Laura managed to survive the selections.

They remained in Auschwitz until the end of July 1944, when they were part of a group of women transferred by train to the Dachau concentration camp. The S.S. guards snickered when, upon their arrival, the bar on the cattle car was opened and they saw the women, heads shaven, dressed in striped prisoner clothing. *Ve ask for voman, but somebody make a mistake and sent to us men,* the guards said. As my mother recounted their words, she had a wry smile on her face.

When I later searched the JewishGen website for additional records of the Perlsteins of Dámóc, I found more details about my mother and Laura's arrival at Dachau. As I read their two names in print in the Dachau concentration camp records — Laura Perlstein and

Szidonia Perlstein — I shivered with a combination of anticipation and anxiety. The facts that followed their names brought many images, more tangible ones, of my mother and her sister's plight as tortured captives. I imagined myself in that railroad car when the bar was opened upon arrival at Dachau, and I felt their fear in not knowing what was in store at yet another camp, having already experienced the agony of the previous one.

Indeed, as the Dachau records show, the two arrived on August 1, 1944, which happened to be a Tuesday that year. The records list Laura Perlstein as having been born on "January 6, 1914, in Samor [sic], Prisoner #86,795" and categorized as a "Hungarian Jew" in "protective custody." My mother's date of birth is listed as "February 28, 1915, born in Damor [sic], Prisoner #86,794," category: "protective custody, Hungarian Jew."

Although I knew much of their Dachau experiences from my mother's accounts, several items proved illuminating. I noted several things: first, the different birth year indicated for my mother in contrast to the one printed on her driver's license, February 28, 1919; second, that my mother and her sister had kept close together up to that point, as evidenced by their prisoner numbers, only one digit apart, similar to their Auschwitz numbers; and third, the "protective custody" designation assigned by the Nazis as one would refer to felons who require special care to protect them from harm, as though they were not slave laborers constantly exposed to injury and death. Moreover, although my mother had always told me that she remembered leaving Dachau in November, the records show that she remained there a month longer, departing on "December 17, 1944," which I have learned was the start of a bitter cold winter in Europe.

Their assignment for the first few months was a small work detail of only about twenty women who were escorted each day to the Dachau palace, or *Schloss*. Surrounded by a beautiful English garden, this historic baroque castle, a favorite home of Bavarian kings and nobility, was set on a hilltop with panoramic views of the town of Dachau, nearby Munich, and of the Alps. Although a large portion of the castle had been destroyed in the nineteenth century, the remaining section still featured a long main hall, known for its banquet facilities and Renaissance wood-coffered ceilings. It had been taken over by the Wehrmacht, the German armed forces, with only a small civilian staff. The work group of women prisoners was to help the staff with cooking and cleaning the enormous palace.

To reach the palace, the women had to walk a couple of miles from the concentration camp. Hoping to blend the women in with the town folk, the camp guards gave them civilian clothes, including underwear, their own underwear having been forcibly shed with the rest of their clothes at Auschwitz, and real shoes to take the place of their wooden clogs. My mother described the following scene, which took place a few weeks after starting the *Schloss* detail:

> *Vhen da weader became cooler, dey gave us coats to vear outside. All of a sudden, Laurie say to anoder voman in our group, 'You are vearing my coat.'*
>
> *Da voman say, 'Vhat you mean I am vearing your coat. Da guards give me dis coat.'*
>
> *'I mean you are vearing my coat from home.'*
>
> *'I don't understand how dis could be your coat from home. Ve are in Dachau.'*
>
> *'I recognize my own coat since I made it mit mine own hands, an I can prove it.'*
>
> *'Okay, show me,' da voman say, removing da coat from her body.*
>
> *Den, you von't believe dis, but Laurie grab da coat by da*

collar and begin to remove da stitches mit her teet an nails. Betveen da interfacing and da outside material vas a few pengo of Hungarian money.

'Dere,' Laurie said, 'dat is how I know it is my coat.'

Da voman stare at Laurie, shaking her head, but know dat she is right, and gave her da coat.

As a child, I always found this story amazing because the coat had miraculously traveled from Auschwitz to Dachau and wound up in the hands of the person who had made it. But these days, I view it as an example of how a skillful seamstress used her talent and ingenuity to try to save her life. That the Hungarian pengo found in the coat collar was an obsolete currency after the war, and possibly close to worthless at the time, is irrelevant. It was key in demonstrating how a seamstress's skill and foresight became more valuable than gold during the Holocaust.

I wonder whether Laura had thought, when she left her home, that the pengo she had sewn into the interfacing of her coat would be traded for some other dear commodity, perhaps for food, transportation, or a passport. Instead, that pengo and the coat formed a precious connection to a time when her family was still united and the coat provided her with warmth for the impending winter.

During their time at the *Schloss*, the civilian staff updated my mother and Laura on the progress of the war. The Allies had landed at Normandy in the previous June, Soviet troops had liberated their first concentration camp at Majdanek in Poland in July, and the mass transports from Hungary to Auschwitz had already been halted. Paris and Bucharest had been liberated in August, and Allied troops had crossed the Siegfried Line and entered Germany in September. For the first time since they had left home, my mother and Laura were encouraged by what they were hearing. My mother recounted the words of their co-workers: *Just a little bit longer and the var vill be over. You vill see. You vill be home soon.* But it was not soon enough.

In September or October of 1944, the two sisters were taken off the Schloss detail and transferred to a Dachau subcamp named Kaufering. With the escalation of Allied air attacks, the German Armaments Ministry attempted to accelerate the construction of massive underground factories, building eleven Kaufering sub-camps where slave laborers worked to perpetuate the German war machine. They housed the laborers in earthen huts, which were covered with sod to disguise them from enemy aircraft. My mother seemed to remember the huts in Kaufering more than in any other camp and sometimes acted out how they entered the underground quarters.

Ve took tree steps down to get inside da block and vere surrounded by dirt floors and valls. Remember, tree steps down. As she said this, she picked up her knees and simulated walking downstairs, as though to ensure I would always recollect her words.

The assignment for the laborers was to work with a crew unloading steel rods from trains. The steel was then taken to an underground installation that appeared to be built right into the side of a mountain. My mother never saw the inside of the factory, but she had heard rumors among the prisoners that they were making arms for the German war effort.

One day, while unloading, my mother lifted a steel rod and lost her balance. The rod landed on her right shin, probably causing a bone fracture. Unable to continue her work, she was taken inside the barracks. She and Laura wondered that night whether she would be able to withstand the roll call the next morning, since she could not stand on her injured leg for more than a minute or two, and then only with great effort.

In the morning, my mother showed up for roll call, still not sure how she would manage to stand, but within a few seconds, one of the guards asked whether any of the prisoners could sew. My mother's hand shot up. She yelled out heartily in German, *Ich, Ich, Ich cann nähen!* Me, me, I can sew! I can envision her screaming out those words with such a powerful voice as to crowd out any sewing rivals, who were most certainly among the other women prisoners. The guard immediately shouted, *You, report to the administration building, now!*

After reporting to the administration building, my mother told me that she never had to go out again, never had to report for roll call, and never returned to the steel construction detail. She quickly adapted to the life of a seamstress in Dachau, of all unlikely places. Soldiers, officers, clerks — males and females — began to bring various odd jobs, like sewing on buttons, repairing ripped seams, mending socks, and replacing broken zippers, all jobs that were done by hand. She had never seen a zipper before since it was a modern convenience, unknown to the residents of her little Hungarian village, so she had to call upon her sewer's instinct to do the job properly. Many years later, when she and I talked about this episode again, she commented, *Pay me a million if I could do dat now,* referring to the hand-sewn zippers, which were so much easier to sew by machine after her arrival in America.

My mother never told me what happened to Laura during the sewing period in Dachau. I know only that she remained alive and that they had met one of their cousins, Olga, who was the daughter of their mother's sister Zali. Olga was a prisoner who happened to work in the kitchen. One evening, Laura and my mother stopped in front of Olga while waiting in line for their watery soup. My cousin Steve, Olga's son, once told me that his mother was trained never to look up while serving food in the concentration camp's soup line in order to avoid any eye contact with the recipients and to ensure that she let the meat stay at the bottom of the pot. She put the ladle in the pot, drew up the broth, and deposited it in my mother's bowl, but my mother did not move on. She stood there until Olga finally looked up at her, cousin to cousin. No one spoke, but Olga, immediately recognizing my mother, returned the ladle into the soup to draw up some meat from the bottom of the pot. *I didn't vant da vaser* [water], *Hani. I vant to have da meat,* my mother related, with a tone of resolve still in her voice.

My mother and Laura left Dachau on that Sunday, December 17, 1944, and were sent on a train to the Bergen Belsen concentration camp. My mother never described any work detail or roll call at Bergen Belsen. By that time, the Allied forces were advancing deeper into Germany, and prisoners from other camps were moved by foot or by train westward. Bergen Belsen was a camp where prisoners from other camps were evacuated, most of them too sick to perform physical labor. She described it as a place where people only went to die.

Winter was setting in, and soon the landscape was filled with dense snow in well-below-freezing temperatures. My mother never said whether they had changed back to their striped clothing once finished with the *Schloss* detail in Dachau, but she vividly remembered the sensation of wandering through ice and snow in clothes that were ragged and thin. Her body, hands, and feet, which at first felt the burn of direct contact with the elements, became numb. Even the barracks were not much of a refuge from the cold, since none was equipped with heaters.

In early 1945, as Bergen Belsen swelled with thousands of new prisoners under deplorable sanitary conditions, typhus raged in epic proportions. Almost no one was exempt from its voracity. The telltale lice, whose feces were responsible for transmitting the disease, could be found almost everywhere on the prisoners' bodies: face and neck, armpits, chest, back, buttocks, and groin. Lice invaded every corner of the barracks and every bunk, each of which was shared by several prisoners at a time. To my mother, Bergen Belsen and lice were synonymous.

By February 1945, both sisters where heavily infested with lice and suffered from typhus. The beautiful but delicate Laura, who somehow managed to survive all the hardships at Auschwitz and Dachau, now had hallucinations.

She only talk about home, and she vant just a single piece of toast, but how ve gonna get toast in Bergen Belsen?

When I was a child and an adolescent, my mother told me the following version of what ultimately happened to Laura:

Ve vere outside our block, vhen Laurie drop down to da ground. I bend down to shake her, to talk to her, to help her to stand up. Her face look up at me. Lice vere crawling around her eyes and mout. I keep looking at her face, even vhen I know she is not breading. I can't take my eyes from her face. I stay dere outside mit her for a vhile, just looking at her, an I hold her.

I have always thought that the turning point in my mother's life, what led her to make some of her decisions and to take certain actions after the war, was Laura's death. They had clung to each other, each helping the other to survive the cruelty and depravity that confronted them in three concentration camps, and then one of them was gone. No one was left to give my mother advice, provide familial support, or stop her from doing stupid things. She was on her own from that point forward.

Typhus continued to rage throughout the camp, where up to sixty thousand people were imprisoned during the last months of the war in Europe. Later, in February, or perhaps in early March of 1945, my mother encountered another resident of her barracks, whose lice-infested body, according to my mother, already foretold her impending death:

A young girl came to me to ask if I can vash her sweater and dress, vhich vas full of lice. I ask her name and vhere she is from, and she say, Anna Frank fun Holland. I tell her I have a sister who marry a man name Frankfurt. Is your name Frankfurt? She say no, her name is Frank. I tell her I vill vash her clothes if she give me her bread. She say she is not hungry, dat I can have her bread. So I vash her clothes in da sink by our block and hang dem up near our beds. She sit on da ground mit a blanket on her. Maybe a veek later, dey pull her out from our block, toyt [dead].

Like the rest of the world, I had read *The Diary of Anne Frank.* When my mother first told me this little story, I wondered whether the girl my mother had described as being in her barracks at Bergen Belsen could have been the Anne Frank whose hidden journal had portrayed the horror of the Holocaust like no other literary work had. It was impossible to know whether the girl whose clothes my mother had washed and the famous Anne Frank were one and the same.

When I asked her, *Do you think that girl may have been the same Anne Frank that the world has come to know and love?* she replied, *To tell you da trut, Hani, it vouldn't change anyting. Vhen ve vere in Bergen Belsen, I just tink she vas von of us, no different.*

I do not know how my mother struggled through the remaining two months without her sister until the Bergen Belsen camp was liberated by the British army on Sunday, April 15, 1945. When the British troops arrived, Yuri, her *Blockalteste,* barracks leader, implored her, *Get up, Szidi, your liberators are here. Get up!* My mother did not answer her. She told me it took a while for her to get out of her bunk to face her liberation. All sense of time was obscured by her weakened body, suspended in a state of otherworldliness, a body and spirit that had been clipped deliberately and decisively numerous times — the way the seam allowance of a heavy fabric is clipped along a curve to force the seam to lay flat — in an attempt to subdue her firm resolve to survive.

18 Equipment

*A craftsman is no better than his tools. — "Equipment,"
page 64*

After having been away at school for four years, I returned
home to Springfield in the summer of 1968. I had been accepted at the University of Connecticut as a graduate student, and
in order to save money on room and board, I decided to live at
home and make the hour's commute from Springfield to Storrs
several days a week. My mother was pleased to have me home
again, even though for only a short time.

Her sewing business had really picked up while I was in college, and by the time I returned home, she had a steady stream of
customers climbing up the steep flight of stairs to her second floor
apartment. My mother greeted and watched each one from the
head of the stairs as though spotting them in case they fell. She
then brought them into her sewing room, equipped with all the
latest tools to enhance the sewer's job.

Her well-padded ironing board was permanently in the "up"
position then, and the Köhler sewing machine was piled high with
patterns and fabric while she used the Pfaff for sewing. While both
sewing machines were originally manufactured with attached
treadles, they had been converted to motorized machines soon
after their arrival in America, allowing for much easier and faster
completion of my mother's sewing assignments. An old kitchen
table served as her cutting board, with various scissors available

for her use: solid-steel dressmaker's shears for cutting fabric; light trimmers for thread; scissors for cutting paper patterns; and pinking shears to keep seams from raveling. They were all either on the table's surface or tucked away in her sewing machine drawer. Pins and threads were strewn not only all over her sewing room floor, but on the living room and bedroom floors as well, hiding among the brown-spice fibers of her rug.

Each customer brought a sewing project to share with her: an idea for a new pantsuit, which had become ever more popular, a dress with matching jacket, a jumper, a blouse, a skirt, a tunic, a ripped seam, or an alteration to make a garment shorter, longer, wider, or narrower. Most of all, I noticed a buzz in my mother's apartment that had never existed when she and I lived together before. Excitement was evident on the faces of both my mother and her customers about the impending completion of their garments. Cozy conversation flowed freely, like that between a hairdresser and her client, where sometimes the patron reveals more about her personal life than she had intended.

You know, Mrs. Perlstein, my husband wanted me to go on a diet because I gained so much weight and I couldn't fit into my clothes anymore, but I just haven't been able to do it, I heard one customer blurt out when I was sitting on the living room sofa facing the door to my mother's sewing room, minding my own business.

Dat's okay. Vhen you lose da veight, ve gonna take it in again, my mother responded with a devilish smile, referring to the skirt waist and side seams that had to be let out significantly.

Oh, Mrs. Perlstein, you're so comforting! You're so good to me.

An you a good customer, my mother said through the pins in her teeth.

It's so nice to meet your daughter after all you told me about her, the woman said, glancing my way, her girdle pushing up a midriff bulge that oddly resembled a mushroom cap.

Tank you.

My mother's way of keeping track of the measurements of her numerous customers and specific sewing jobs was to use one of her most important pieces of equipment: a four-by-six-inch spiral notebook. She filled many such notebooks with the vital fashion statistics of everyone for whom she sewed. As I recently perused one of those precious notebooks, I realized that the language she used in her writing was one that almost defied translation. Yet after studying one of the notebooks for many hours with my daughter's help, I finally discerned the method. Each entry was written in English with Hungarian overtones for spelling and pronunciation. Here is an example of a list of my mother's sewing jobs and prices:

Mrs. Godman [Goodman]

Grin penc szut [green pantsuit]	*5.50*
Grin dresz [green dress]	*4.00*
Brun dresz [brown dress]	*4.00*
Veit penc [white pants]	*2.50*
Long szk and top [long skirt and top]	*6.00*
Csek penc [check pants]	*2.50*
Bluse print [print blouse]	*2.50*
Safari szut new [new Safari suit]	*35.00*

The quietness that had marked our life together had been broken by these customers, who looked at my mother with anticipation, appreciation, and genuine affection. They could not hide any secrets about their outward body from her, and sometimes their inner thoughts and fantasies spilled over as well. No one knew

Mrs Jodman
grün penc sut   5.50
grün dress   4.00
brun dr.   4.00
weit penc   2.50
long sik and top hat 6.00
print hot and dr.   4.00
back print dr.   3.00
grin penc   3.00
... ek penc   2.50
blue socket   2.50
bluse print   2.50
penc and swit   3.50
4 penc   80.00
                     123.00
long dr   3.00
grün socket   2.50
... Kenhom   3.00
                    134.50
bâsiseket   2.50
                    137.00
material   8.00
                    42.00

A page from Sidonia's spiral notebook

more about the seamstress's ability to peer into a person's soul than I did. The master sewer possessed intuitive tools that often I could not escape, no matter how hard I tried.

She was much more adept than I was at holding on to her innermost secrets, usually finding out about most of the secrets I ever had, from dating boys she did not like to neglected homework. Observing my mother's customer interaction, I recalled the time when I was halfway through the first semester of my first year in college. She could tell that I was not paying much attention to my studies, enthralled by the independence of college life. My disappointing mid-semester grades confirmed what she had sensed. One night, she took the car trip from Springfield to Amherst, along the back roads of Routes 5 and 9 before the highway was finished. With my two roommates, Joyce and Sharon, looking on in awe, she burst into my dorm room and read me the riot act about my ingratitude for all she had sacrificed to make sure I had a good education, her face flushed with rage.

> *Hani, vhy you go to college if you gonna make such low marks?*
>
> *Ma, you shouldn't have come here like this.*
>
> *Vhy not? I am your moder. If not me, den who else? Tell me, who else?*
>
> *I don't know ma. I don't know.*
>
> *So, Hani, vhat you gonna do about it?*
>
> *I'll do better, ma. You'll see that my grades at the end of the semester will be better.*
>
> *Okay, Hani. Ve'll see, ve'll see. If dey not better, den you just come home for good. You shouldn't be in college.*
>
> *Okay, ma, okay,* I replied through my intense sobbing.

Throughout her scolding, my head was tilted downward, the tears rolling down my face onto my lips, making it even more difficult for me to speak in my defense. I never saw her leave. I heard only the loud thud of her slamming the door shut, leaving all of us in dead silence, stunned by what had just happened.

My mother's cold stare was usually sufficient to straighten me out, but this was different. Education meant more to her than it did to me at the time. She was determined that I would not be a seamstress like her, even though my lack of talent made that highly improbable anyway. My fate, already planned since we had arrived in America, was a college education and a white-collar profession, at least until I married. I was ashamed of my mother's unexpected outburst in front of my new college friends yet curiously amazed at her keen instincts. Her vituperative rant had the intended result of forcing me to focus on my academics for fear of angering her any further.

Now I was back home at age twenty-one and taking the lonely journey to the University of Connecticut almost every day. Her eruption about my grades back when I was a college first-year student was a distant memory at that point, my head fixed firm-ly on my studies. However, as a commuting student, I never had much opportunity to interact with my fellow classmates, and in my mother's home, where we were rarely able to share amusing conversation, I longed for social connections to alleviate the lone-liness.

I renewed my friendship with a young man two years my senior from Hartford whom I had known since I was sixteen, when the Hartford and Springfield Jewish teens routinely met at dances, parties, and the Connecticut shoreline. Together we went on long car rides, the movies, and informal dinners. When we announced our engagement a year later, my mother was not too surprised but delighted at my choice of a husband. Bruce met her expectations of a man who was worthy of her daughter. He was an attractive, self-employed businessman with prospects of wealth in the future: he listened when she spoke; and he was very tall. Perhaps he reminded her of her parents and siblings back home in Hungary, who, she always told me, were tall — especially her brother, Dezso. Height seemed to represent protection and comfort to her. Although by then I had left home to take a teaching job in Connecticut while I continued to complete my master's studies, the stability inferred by my upcoming marriage seemed to set well with her. *I gonna call him my son, not my son-in-law,* she said, *because he feel like a son to me.*

A linen tunic top and matching bell bottoms a few months before the author's wedding

The wedding was scheduled for December 28, 1969, only eight weeks after we announced our intentions. Although I knew my mother expected me to marry some day, a fancy wedding was never part of our conversations and not something I dreamed of or expected. When the time came, eight weeks was plenty of time to plan for our fifty guests and a low-key ceremony and reception at Park Manor, where the Club Hatikvah used to hold its special events, but which by the end of the 1960s had long since passed its heyday.

It was the wedding dress that I remember most. It fit the subdued plans of the day, and yet it was a masterpiece. Ever the proponent of elegant, understated simplicity over extravagant and showy designs, my mother brought out her best skills to create her mother-of-the-bride suit and my bridal gown. It did not require numerous fittings. She had again envisioned the dress before ever starting to sew, undertaking the task in a methodical manner. I remember her sitting with her legs stretched out, one crossing the

other, in her usual place on the floor of her sewing room, pincushion and yardstick by her side, her full-length mirror propped up against the wall that divided the room from the front porch. When I was ready to try on the gown, it was already basted at the armholes for the set-in sleeves and at the waist. It required just a few pins at the side seams and around the bodice to fit just right.

Careful not to catch my skin, ma. Treat me like you treat your customers, was the comment that always elicited

The perfect wedding dress

the most raucous laugh from her.

Dey all like to fit better den you, she would invariably reply. But then, getting back to business, she began to look at the hem. *Stand up straight, Hani, odervise da dress vill look crooked,* she reminded me for the millionth time as her eyes wandered up my tall form. I *vant to hem da dress just long enough to cover da top of your shoes.*

Then, as pins emerged from her mouth as automatically as candy from a Pez dispenser, she inserted them horizontally around the skirt of the dress every one or two inches, at the appropriate distance from the floor as measured by her yardstick. When the horizontal pinning was finished, she lifted up the skirt and folded it on the inside at the edge of each pin, planting a vertical pin crosswise to the horizontal one to hold up the hem, offering a preview of the finished skirt length. I often balked at the tedious, boring task of standing for a fitting, but I recall that the wedding gown so excited me that I did not mind standing for the hem or the sleeve length and fit, or checking the belt, or watching my full image reflected in her mirror.

The gown looks great, ma. It feels so light, I beamed as I viewed myself in her mirror, turning from front to side to back.

I vant you to feel very comfort table [her two-word pronunciation for 'comfortable'] *in dis dress. It's your vedding. It's gonna be da best day of your life.*

The gown was made of white satin peau de soie with no trim except for pearl beading affixed to its stand-up collar. In tune with the winter season, it had long blouson sleeves gathered at the wrist into French cuffs and a draped belt made of the same fabric looped into a circular clear crystal buckle. Its skirt hung naturally to the floor with no train or embellishments. A tulle veil that fell just below the back of my waist was attached to a floral white headpiece, topping my long brown hair. Simple yet perfect.

As a steady, fine snow fell outside, I walked down the aisle alone in my homemade bridal gown, the heels of my white shoes clicking on the uncarpeted wood floor. My mother waited for me in her rose pink wool-silk-blend dress and matching jacket, standing with my groom, my one attendant, cousin Olga's daughter, Ann, and the groom's foster parents under the chuppah.

19 Zippers

Before removing old zipper, always examine your garment to see how zipper was put in. Since you must follow the lines of old folds and stitching, you may have to adapt directions to variations in construction. — "Zippers," page 184

Despite the life she herself had led as a single woman, my mother was undeniably a traditionalist when it came to matrimony. Her models for the fundamentals of marriage were her own parents, who had been married for forty-three years when her mother died. I listened closely in my first few years of marriage as my mother gave me her honest advice. Her counsel included the following recommendations:

> Don't forget who is boss: your husband.
> Keep a clean house so everyvon vill tink you are a good baleboste.
> Don't let your husband cook, clean, or vash dishes.
> Never leave dishes in da sink overnight.
> Never go to bed angry.
> Love mean just getting used to each oder.
> Be smart. Do vhat you tink is right.
> Vatch your money.

My mother believed that the role of a wife was to be subservient to her husband when it came to the daily functioning of the household, but she also believed that a woman's instinctive powers to understand the true nature of things made her in many ways superior to her spouse. Her own mother, Hani, was a woman who keenly understood the social, religious, and political dynamics of her little village and took strong action to sustain, nurture, and integrate her family in a country where their faith could have separated them from community involvement and leadership.

Contrary to her desire to see me as a stay-at-home baleboste, economic needs required me to remain in the workforce while my husband continued to build his two-way-radio business. I finished my first master's degree and left my short stint as a social studies teacher in the early 1970s to become a social worker in Connecticut in Hartford's North End, a bastion of alcohol and drug addiction, unemployment, and poverty. I felt strangely comfortable in the environment of the North End, a certain kinship with my fellow workers and with the African American residents of the neighborhood. It surrounded the Northside field office, a small fortress with iron bars on its windows, on the corner of Westland and Barbour Streets.

On a subconscious level, I think it reminded me in some ways of my old neighborhood in Springfield's North End, where *di grine* and their neighbors worked at low-paying jobs and lived in dilapidated surroundings, struggling to survive in a world that had not totally accepted them. *Di grine*, however, had left their despair and misery behind them to assume a spirit of resilience and renewal, yet never forgetting the human tragedies they had endured.

But in 1971, only three years after the death of Martin Luther King, Jr., and the subsequent riots, fires, and destruction of property, vacant lots dotted the North End landscape like a painful psoriasis on human skin, its dispirited residents displaying bitterness and hopelessness. It was there, in the gray, forlorn backdrop of north Hartford that I found my professional calling. For the first time in my life I thought I could really make a difference in people's lives.

If my mother had viewed the scene, I suspect she would have attempted to dissuade me from continuing the work, fearing it too dangerous. I was, at first, overwhelmed by the harsh directness of many of the people with whom I interacted, angry at a system that had left them disheartened and demoralized and who saw me as its representative. After bursting into tears after each client visit in the first week, I overheard some of my superiors through the walls of my partitioned office discussing their grim forecast for my future in the social work profession.

Yeah, she's not going to last long. I'll take bets she doesn't make it even two more weeks.

My face flushed upon hearing their disparaging prognosis, and at that moment, I was overcome by self-doubt and reservations about my professional future. Yet their biting comments only made me fight harder to be accepted as a social worker and to prove to them, and to myself, that I had the fortitude to work in that troubled neighborhood and achieve positive results for the people I served. As I helped to connect young addicts with treatment services and gainful employment, assisted ex-offenders to reenter the community, and secured financial benefits for families and the elderly, I became more confident in my ability to improve the world in some small way.

The job, more than anything else up to that point, helped me to discard the insulated, pampered, and egocentric yet shy human being I had inadvertently become as the sole focus of a mother's desire to demonstrate to the world that she existed, she had survived, and had produced a perfect daughter. I was finally able to step out of my personal boundaries and became a stronger, more socially responsive, and compassionate person. Starting in the 1970s, I was striving for perfection not just in my outward demeanor and appearance, but in my newfound vocation as a catalyst for social change. As I think back on it, perhaps the stage had been set for me all along by my mother's stories of social injustice and oppression and their effects on human behavior. Without my conscious awareness, my developing talent as a patient listener of her mesmerizing tales proved to be my finest social work training.

Yet all the while I was working in north Hartford, and for many years after that, I was still my mother's daughter in the fashion sense. It had become a way of life. In spite of becoming ever more sensitized to class disparity by working with the poor, I continued to display my mother's beautiful couture designs at the office. Although I was representing the House of Perlstein and not the House of Dior, I must have looked as though I had spent a fortune on my personal attire. Seeming to reflect the affluent while serving the indigent was a contradiction lost on me at the time.

For the first two years of my work in Hartford, respectful of my mother's need to produce her usual high volume of handmade garments and perfectly willing to comply, I wore a succession of homemade outfits without repetition to the amazement of my co-workers and probably my clients. Brown tweed suits, black wool skirts with scotch plaid blazers, peach silk blouses with big tied bows, purple crepe skirts with matching jackets, cotton miniskirts with vests, polyester or silk sleeveless shells in a variety of colors, Eisenhower jackets with matching wide pants, and the classic Chanel suit in salt and pepper wool edged with black piping were among the jewels in my wardrobe. After four hundred and eighty workdays of this marathon, I finally gave up, never repeating this feat again, but forever averse to wearing the same outfit within too short an interval.

If work was a first step away from my self-centeredness, in 1974 I took the second step: the birth of my daughter, Brenda. We decided not to tell my mother when I began labor for fear it would overburden her with anxiety, so we waited to tell her of the baby's birth when it was all over. I had never been around babies or small children before, so it was an education and wondrous joy to have a beautiful baby girl. Her playful yet headstrong, determined nature began at birth and continues to this day, a disposition that appealed to my heart at once. My mother, overcome with excitement, said she reminded her of Szeren, her outspoken, assertive oldest sibling, but I think she was secretly reminded of her own resolute personality.

Yet in those early years as a mother, I could never put myself in my own mother's shoes to wonder about or identify with the feelings she must have had when she gave birth to me. I never thought about her emotions during her pregnancy or after giving birth to a baby girl alone in a displaced persons camp. Her inability to let her guard down and loosen her intransigence about sharing the truth of my conception left us with a partition between us as solid as any wall. I still held on to a deep anger toward her that made it impossible to connect any of my personal experiences with those she may have endured.

Meanwhile, I continued my work in Hartford through the rest of the 1970s, raising our daughter and achieving a second master's degree, this time in social work. My mother was content to drive the twenty miles from Springfield to visit us every Sunday when we bought a home in Vernon, a suburban community twelve miles east of the capital city of Hartford. She fell in love instantly with the house and its half acre of land, considering it partially hers since she had made the purchase possible with her gift of a down payment. But her behavior changed after my marriage and sharpened with the birth of our daughter. She had become more anxious and obsessive about our safety and security. She imagined each of us in our daily activities from the moment we awoke in the morning until we went to bed at night. She phoned every evening to ask how I was, shortening my name to "Han," pronouncing it 'Hahn,' after my marriage.

>*Han, how you? I vas tinking about you all day, vondering how you driving on a day like dis.*
>
>*Ma, it's only a little rain. Everyone is fine, really.*
>
>*So everyvon is home now?*
>
>*Yes, everyone is home.*
>
>*Vell, don't go out again tonight. Du solst blaybn ahaym* [You should stay at home].
>
>*Okay, don't worry. We're staying home tonight,* I would reply, even if I had other plans.

I was reduced to the occasional fib or outright lie in order to keep her mind at peace, repeating this same dialogue many times over the next thirty years. Though I never remembered her as anxious or watchful when I was younger, as our family grew larger, I believe she felt she was no longer in control the way she was when it was only me she had to think of. Additional family members seemed overwhelming to her, too unwieldy to contain within her imagined parameters, as memories of a previous family were still pervasive in her dreams and thoughts. She had lost one family, and she could not bear to lose another.

In turn, my mother also withheld the truth, about many things. I discovered another example of this in the mid 1970s. On one of her visiting Sundays, she pulled me aside as my daughter was taking a nap and in a quiet, sincere tone said:

>*Han, you know, I vas tinking. I might be born in a different year den 1919.*
>
>*What are you talking about, ma?* I asked, not quite understanding.

Vell, I vas just tinking dat maybe I vas born a little earlier.
Don't you know how old you are, ma?
Yeh, I know, but sometime I'm not sure, she replied in
the most obfuscating manner possible.
What makes you think of this now?
I don't know vhy, but ve should check to see da date. Maybe
ve can find my birt certificate.

She had used the birth date of February 28, 1919, for as long as
I had known her. It was the official date on her visa documents,
her citizenship papers, her driver's license, medical records, and
anything else bearing her name and vital statistics. Born in a tiny
village, she had no idea where her birth certificate was located or
even whether it still existed, but she seemed determined to find it.

Establishing her date of birth proved easier than we had anticipated. We decided to contact Congressman Edward Boland, the
well-known, longtime representative from western Massachusetts.
His office contacted the Hungarian embassy in Washington, D.C.,
which quickly found and forwarded my mother's birth certificate.
It had been housed in Miskolc, the capital city of the now-merged
county of Borsod-Abaúj-Zemplén. The following information was
stated on a white four- by six-inch folded card. Translated from the
Hungarian, it read:

Perlstein Szidonia, an infant girl, was born on February
27, 1913, in the village of Dámóc. Father: Perlstein, Simon.
Profession: saloonkeeper, resident of Dámóc. Mother: Klein,
Hani, also a resident of Dámóc.

I was thunderstruck when I read the date of my mother's birth.
Not only was the birth year six years earlier than the date she had
officially circulated to every public institution with whom she had

interacted in the United States, but the day was also different. I felt betrayed and confused by this new information. Why would she have deliberately deceived everyone in this country, including her own daughter? What could have been her motive?

Upon reading the newly uncovered birth certificate, my mother seemed to accept the stated facts easily, as though she had known them all along. As usual, she did not feel the need to add much explanation other than that the reason stemmed from her wartime experiences. Without telling her, I felt cheated out of six years of her life. Perhaps she was six years closer to death and I would lose her earlier than expected, the one person who had been my family before my marriage. It was 1975 when my mother was inspired to search for proof of her birth, which meant she was then sixty-two instead of fifty-six. I do not believe it was a coincidence that her discovery coincided with her eligibility for Social Security benefits.

Only after her death did I understand how the age deception began and why it happened. The Dachau concentration camp records show the dates of birth of my mother and her sister Laura while interned at Dachau. Both had given false birth dates. Laura's was listed as "January 6, 1914," and my mother's as "February 28, 1915." The ruse may have begun even earlier at Auschwitz as they underwent examinations naked by Dr. Mengele and his team of "doctors." Fearful that her varicose veins may have marked her for death, my mother may have begun to falsify her age to offset this detrimental physical ailment, and Laura may have followed suit. The reality, then, since Laura was older than my mother, was that Laura must have been born before 1913, my mother's birth year.

JewishGen shows my mother's name listed in a 1945 Hungarian periodical *Hirek az Elhurcoltakrol* (News about the Deportees) already displaying 1919 as her year of birth, Damo [sic] as her birth city, and her location as the Bergen Belsen displaced persons camp.

So it appears that sometime between her registration at Dachau and her liberation at Bergen Belsen, she had decided to further decrease her age.

My mother's opportunity to establish the earlier birth date occurred after the war at Camp Wentorf, the visa processing camp. In lieu of a birth certificate, two witnesses — one born in Budapest, the other in Szabadka, neither of which are anywhere near Dámóc — attested to her date of birth as being February 28, 1919. Remembering that her mother had often joked about her birth being close to February 29, which would have been a lucky day had it been a leap year, she may have altered the exact day without even noticing it.

Without a birth certificate to prove otherwise, my mother was able to pass as six years younger than her true age, starting with her visa to gain entrance to the United States. Coming to America at the age of thirty instead of thirty-six offered her greater advantages regarding gainful employment and social acceptance. I just wish she could have shared this precious secret with me.

20 Backstitch

Backstitch makes strong seams. Bring needle and thread out on stitching line. Take a stitch back about ⅟₁₆", bringing needle out ⅛" forward (i.e., ⅟₁₆ inch from where you first came out). To continue, keep putting your needle in at end of last stitch and bringing it out one stitch ahead. — "Hand-Sewing," page 97

The Perlstein family home, Dámóc, Hungary. The sign over the door reads Elelm-iszer (Grocery Store)

1983. I gave birth to a second child in 1980, Stephen, a boy so adventurous and imaginative he could break down a telephone to its parts when he was barely a year old, and when he was less than two, hide his parents' keys because he knew it would surely torment them. My mother said he reminded her of her brother, Dezso, the rascal. That same year, I took a job as the director of Human Services in Manchester, Connecticut, staying in the field that I had grown to love in Hartford. It marked the beginning of a decade of family and career growth for me, but also one of personal revelation.

As my mother approached her seventieth birthday, I thought that if I were ever to see Dámóc, the town that had spawned her idyllic childhood, I would have to do it soon, since I was not sure how much longer she would have the will or the stamina to take such a long trip. I could never envision visiting the small village without her; it had always seemed so elusive to me, so very far away in time and place. I needed her to revisit her own experiences with me to attach physical reality to my inadequate fantasy. For so many years, it was only my mother's voice that had described the little community that was Dámóc. I longed to see it for myself.

August 1983, the year my mother turned seventy, and the month in which I turned thirty-six, was time to make the pilgrimage. She agreed to the trip without hesitation, even with a hint of eagerness, perhaps hoping finally to revisit the place where she had experienced the happiest of times. We decided to take my nine-year-old daughter, Brenda, along with us. Requesting two weeks' vacation from my job, I left three-year-old Stephen with his father as we took our leave for Hungary. We arrived at the airport in Budapest with plans to meet my mother's first cousin Ferenc there.

It had been almost forty years since the cousins had seen each other, and each had changed much with age. We walked the length of the airport several times in frustration, passing him more than once before my mother and he were both struck by recognition. Feri, as he was called, wore a short-sleeved white shirt and dark pants, his tousled hair as gray as my mother's, his eyes somewhat mournful below his bushy gray eyebrows.

They both fell into each other's arms and began to talk energetically in Hungarian — their mouths moving too quickly for me to come even close to comprehension — relief on their faces. As Feri helped my mother with her suitcase, he asked us to stop for a moment at a phone booth to call his wife, yet again, apparently having called her numerous times during our missed encounters, to ask her whether she had heard from us. He advised her that we had finally found one another and all was well. We had not missed our plane after all. Feri's wife must have asked, *How does Szidi look?* I heard him respond: *Just as I remember.* Feri drove us in his Soviet-made automobile to his home in Miskolc, then the third largest city in Hungary, where we stayed with him and his wife, Sevi, for the next week, visiting with his family and sightseeing.

Our tour included the Miskolc Tapolca, where we soaked in the ancient soothing thermal cave baths, and Lillafured, the lush resort nestled in the nearby Bukk Mountains. I was impressed by the beauty and grandeur of the northeast region of Hungary, where my ancestors had made their home over many generations. After our tour, however, cousin Feri had only one day still available to take the two-hour trip to Dámóc, so we had limited time to take in all that we wanted to see in my mother's hometown.

On the morning we set out from Miskolc, we sat in the back seat as Feri drove at speeds near race car levels. He impatiently passed other cars, swerved away from horse-drawn carriages still dotting country roads, and generally drove as though he were in a frantic rush, all of which served to heighten my anxiety about finally seeing the place where my mother had been born and raised.

My mother spoke Hungarian during our visit, speaking English only when conversing directly with Brenda and me or when interpreting Hungarian for us. Our English conversation in that back seat between grandmother, daughter, and granddaughter sounded something like this:

Han, your cousin drive like a crazy, whispered my mother as she braced herself by clutching at the front passenger seat, *but I very excited dat ve almost in Dámóc.*

And then, turning toward the driver, *Feri, why are you driving so fast?* She asked this with a critical voice in Hungarian; no interpretation for me needed. Feri mumbled something under his breath, as though we Americans could not possibly understand the rules of Hungarian driving.

I tugged on my mother's arm and said, *Listen, ma, I just want to remind you of what we need to accomplish today. We need to find your house and then go inside to see if we can find the jewelry,* referring to the hidden box inside the hearth, inserted there by her family the night before they had left their home forever.

I had formulated two goals for my mission to Dámóc. The first was just simply to see the village and my mother's family home. Second, I wanted to find the jewelry, not because of any monetary value, but because I hoped it would give me some tangible evidence that once there was a real family of which my mother was a part, that my grandmother's finger had once held a certain gold wedding ring, and my grandfather had worn a certain watch, handed down through the generations, in his vest pocket. Having some of their possessions, I believed, would bring me closer to them and give me a sense of belonging to my family.

Yeh, Hani, yeh, ve gonna see if ve can find da jewelry, but I really vant just to see my house, she responded.

I turned to my daughter, who was sitting quietly and looking out the window: *What are you thinking about Brenda?*

I'm thinking that I feel just like Nancy Drew in one of her mysteries, she answered eagerly. No wonder that Nancy Drew, the great fictional teen detective, was on her mind. We had been reading

The Hidden Staircase together at night during our trip and had just reached the part where Nancy pushed the knob inside the dark closet, and suddenly, the side of the closet wall dropped down, revealing a hidden passageway.

I gazed out the car window myself and noticed the gently rolling hills and peaceful river valleys of the northeastern countryside. As we passed Tokaj, the historic wine country near my grandmother's birthplace at the juncture of the Bodrog and Tisza Rivers, I observed the vast rows of lush verdant grapevines as far as my eye could see. I envisioned my grandmother's family busy with the production of wine as their ancestors had since at least the mid-nineteenth century — planting, tending, harvesting, and fermenting the grapes that resulted in some of the finest white wines in the world.

We continued to travel northeast toward Dámóc, stopping to eat in Sárospatak, a center of Jewish learning in my mother's time. We all ordered fish soup, which turned out to be a steamy, brothy mixture brimming with fragments of fish and assorted green vegetables, completely satisfying our appetites. Then we journeyed on for another hour into the blazing hot early afternoon until we saw the green streetlike sign pointing to Dámóc.

My pulse was racing as we entered *Fö Utca*, Main Street, the center of the six-hundred-year-old village. We had been on a paved road into town, which had been only dirt when my mother left it, for less than a minute when my mother, whose eyes were darting from side to side in anticipation of some sign to prod her memory, shouted to Feri, *Stop the car, please!* She had spotted a man she recognized dressed in gray, wool pants and a short-sleeved white shirt. As Feri stopped the car, she quickly leaped out of the back seat and approached the man, who had been walking down the street but had stopped abruptly as he saw this woman come toward him, perhaps even calling him by name. We could not hear them talking, and my mother had her back to us, but the man's face turned ashen, and with an incredulous look, he pointed up the street, apparently explaining where to find her house. She thanked him and calmly turned away, returning to the car's back seat and motioning to Feri to keep driving straight ahead.

Traveling slowly up the street, we observed the unassuming exteriors of the cement-and-plaster houses we passed, many of them set behind wrought-iron gates. Colorful dahlias, petunias, and marigolds in front of each one stood in stark contrast with the drab facades, offering a break from the monotony. The main street of the bucolic village seemed empty except for the man we had encountered earlier, which lulled us into thinking perhaps we would not see anyone else during our visit. Soon we were pulling up to my mother's house, which was on the right side of *Fö Utca*.

There it was, the house she had left in such haste almost forty years before, built on what was then the new extension of the street, back in the 1930s. It was a rather sturdy boxlike structure made of cement, covered with tan paint, and topped with a terra cotta mansard roof. Its foundation extended upward, almost to the bottom rim of the three front windows. A small sign at the crest of the light-green iron double doors read *Elelmiszer*, grocery store, but it looked dark inside and barren on the exterior. There were no flowers adorning its front as we had seen on other houses, yet we noticed that behind the house lay acres of farmland with rows of corn, wheat, and apple trees.

No one spoke for the next few minutes as we all emerged from the car and watched my mother walk up the five front stairs to the double doors and knock. No sound came from within the house. The doors were locked. Brenda pointed her Polaroid camera at the house and began to shoot while I fumbled with my 35-mm camera, my hands visibly shaking. All of us then followed my mother as she went around to the side of the house, and I noticed that while the front gave the appearance of a somewhat commercial edifice, the side revealed tall, dried, long-faded flowers crowded around another entrance, like the remnant of a well-planned garden. The side door had the appearance of a French patio portal, unlike the rigid front doors, but it, too, was locked.

Sidonia approaches the side door of her family's home

I felt an immense wave of disappointment at our discouraging initial attempts at gaining entrance to the house and thought we would have to leave the little town without ever seeing the inside of my mother's family home, or of having a chance to search for the jewelry. I turned to my mother and spoke the first words since we entered the village.

What should we do now, ma? It looks like this house has been abandoned, I moaned.

I don't know Hani, but let's see if ve can find somevon to ask, she responded, maintaining the calm she had exhibited up to that point.

She spun around. Directly across the street, behind a chain-link fence, she saw an elderly woman dressed in a black coat, dark stockings, and gray kerchief, despite the sweltering heat, her slight frame bent over to feed the chickens and geese that wandered freely behind her. My mother motioned us to follow her lead; a hint of recognition lighted her face.

We crossed the street and approached the fence as the woman drew closer to see who these strangers were who had come to visit. My mother introduced herself in Hungarian, *I'm Szidi, one of the Perlsteins who lived across the street many years ago.* When the woman identified herself, my mother immediately fell into quiet tears for the first time. I learned later that her sobs stemmed from the astonishment of seeing this woman so ravaged and stooped by time compared with the fine-looking, tall, upright figure she remembered. The woman, whose face showed little emotion, then invited us to join her inside her house.

Inside, we met her son, a gaunt, tall, angular man, perhaps in his late fifties, sitting on a sofa with a full glass of vodka in his hand, somewhat inebriated from a morning's worth of drinking. I observed that the room in which he sat seemed to center around the kitchen, which had a water faucet with a pail underneath but no sink. A wood table and chairs were in the center of the room, surrounded by beds, all covered with thick feather comforters that were topped with woven tapestry spreads decorated with white crocheted doilies.

Christian religious symbols, such as dolls of the baby Jesus, sat on top of the beds, and crucifixes were mounted on the walls around the sleeping area. A modern television set, the only concession to a contemporary, technological world, was located in a corner. The room was basic and compact yet functional, not complicated by phones, kitchen appliances, or separate bedrooms and baths, as we are accustomed to having in America.

My mother and Feri both fell into a vigorous discussion with the woman and her son as they all sat down beside one another on the sofa. With my limited Hungarian, I could barely keep up with the conversation. My mother, now animated and leaning on the son's arm, tried to interpret. Here's the part of her monologue that stuck in my head:

> *He ask me if I remember who take us to Ricse vhen ve leave our house.*
> *I say no.*
> *He say it vas him. Da gendarmes ask him da night before if he have a horse an vagon to use, and he say yes.*
> *He vas afraid to tell dem no.*

I was astounded at my mother's words, but she continued to engage this man in conversation as though his admission and bit of memory meant little to her. The departure from her home that fateful morning in 1944 and journey to Ricse, a nearby village and gathering point for Jews on their way to the ghetto, had been facilitated by this man sitting beside her. She had been unable to recount that fact for years, and now, in an instant, it was elucidated. I was amazed that she was able to continue, as though this piece of information was unimport-
ant. It was not until many years later that I realized that block-ing out this picture, like many others, was the only way she was able to maintain her sanity.

Left to right, the first woman met on the author's trip with Sidonia to Dámóc, 1983, with Sidonia and Feri

They told us that my mother's house had current owners, but they were unable to give us any other details. After thanking them for their hospitality, we left to walk up the street to see whether we could find the old Jewish cemetery, and, I hoped, obtain more information about the house's owners. Farther up the road, we encountered two young men and a woman in front of their home.

My mother introduced herself again, and one of the young men, wearing nothing but blue swim trunks, immediately replied, *Of course, I believe my father knew your family very well.*

We would like to see the Jewish cemetery. Can you take us there? she asked.

He nodded, and the entire party, the young man and the two others, whose identities were unclear, my mother, Brenda, Feri, and I traversed wheat, corn, and sunflower fields to find the small Jewish cemetery tucked amid farmland. I was astonished that this graveyard, which held the memories of all the Jews who had perished in this little village, was hidden away in these cornfields, as though it were an abandoned parcel surrounded by the seeds of a world that continued to live and grow, forgetting it ever existed.

The cemetery was in a state of inattention and disarray, probably having received few visitors for several decades. Vegetation had grown so tall that the markers were not visible without pushing it aside, and some of the stones were so eroded that the markings had become difficult to read. The cemetery's sad neglect, combined with our nervousness and inadequate ability to read the Hebrew on the headstones, made it difficult to determine the graves' identities.

However, we were able to discern the grave of my mother's sister Margit, who had died after World War I of the Spanish flu, and then the headstone of my grandmother Hani, recognizing the letters of her Hebrew name, *Chana*, the same as mine. Later, upon showing the photos I had taken of these graves to my rabbi, who could better translate the Hebrew, I learned that the *Chana* whose name appeared on the gravestone was not my grandmother after all, but someone else, the daughter of "Rabbi Yehudah," which was not my great grandfather's name.

Dámóc, the grave mistaken for that of the author's grandmother Hani (Chana)

Our eyes were captivated by one grave marker that stood out from the rest, since at its apex were the wax remnants of two burned candles. It was the grave of my grandfather's sister. We asked our escorts about the candles, and they acknowledged that two young men had visited the village two weeks before our arrival. They had burned the candles and said prayers at the grave, but we had no idea who they were. Meanwhile, our male guides, acting like kids, performed gymnastics, tumbling and somersaulting in the outside perimeter of the cemetery as we conducted our solemn mission.

Upon leaving the graveyard, we asked about the owners of my mother's house. The men told us that one of the owners was currently at the hospital visiting her sick husband but would probably return in an hour or two. They also informed us that one Jewish inhabitant of the town, Bela Marton, had returned after the war and had worked in the store that fronted my mother's house and, furthermore, that she still lived in the nearby town of Zemplénagárd.

I said to my mother, *Ma, here's an idea. Let's visit this Bela and then return to Dámóc. Maybe by then, the owner will have returned and will let us into the house.*

My mother remembered the woman and replied, *Yeh, Hani, I vould like to talk to Bela. Feri, let's go to Zemplénagárd!*

We traveled a couple of miles to Zemplénagárd and surprised Bela Marton as she opened her front door. My mother had only to reveal her name for Bela to reach out to embrace her. She was a widow who also had lost most of her family in the war, but she advised us that she still had two sisters living in Israel. Her house was as modest as the one we had visited in Dámóc: a kitchen with one faucet and pail, no sink, and a kitchen table and chairs with a bedroom area surrounding it. She recounted how, upon returning to Dámóc after the war, one of my mother's distant cousins, claiming to be the only survivor of the Perlstein extended clan, laid claim to my mother's family home and its adjoining grocery store. Bela worked there as a clerk for a while. Later, the cousin sold the home to its current owners.

Hearing this news, my mother's face contorted, her lips pursed tightly, and her eyes narrowed as though she were trying to keep from exploding. She kept her composure until we had left Bela's house, when she finally erupted into an emotional tirade about someone who, without checking into possible heirs who might still exist, had usurped the family property.

Dat's vhat I vant to know, Han, she shouted. *Vhy didn't he even try to find me? He just take our house, just like dat. Settle down, ma. There's nothing we can do about that*

now. Maybe he didn't know how to find you.
   Yeh, Han, he could search for me. He didn't even try.
I gonna find out more about it. It's just wrong.

I was surprised by this turn of events. She had never thought about someone else laying claim to her family home as his own inheritance, but then again, neither did she know that this cousin had survived and returned to the town after the war. But life had gone on in her little village after she left. Property had been acquired and sold, and she was not there to intervene.

We decided to return to Dámóc to see whether the owner had come back from the hospital. As we entered the village this time, we heard the noise of many voices on *Fö Utca*. We wondered what had occurred in the short hour we had been gone. As our car cautiously drove toward my mother's house, we observed many people lining the street and heard the chant, *Szidike, Szidike,* an affectionate form of my mother's name, growing louder and louder. Word had spread among the residents that my mother had returned after so many years, and while we were visiting Bela, they had emerged from their houses in anticipation of our second arrival. At that moment, I felt like the daughter of a local dignitary who had come back to her humble beginnings. I was touched, but somewhat uncertain as to what to make of this welcome.

We stopped the car and left the townspeople outside for the time being as we encountered one of the owners of my mother's house, who had the key in her hand, already understanding that we wished to go inside. She opened the side door of the house, and we entered. The three rooms, excluding the store, were totally dark and empty, no furniture, beds, curtains, or kitchen items. Apparently, no one had occupied the house for quite some time, though we were never told why. We all looked around for a brief moment until I asked my mother in English:

Ma, I don't see a hearth or fireplace in this house. Are you sure there was such a hearth when you left home?

Han, I'm sure. Yes, it vas vhere dis vall is in da kitchen. Somevon cover it up or knock it down.

You know, ma, we're going to knock this wall down and see if there's a brick hearth underneath it, unless the owner stops us. Ask Feri if he has any ideas, I said, firmly convinced that I did not want to leave the town without the jewelry.

My mother whispered something into Feri's ear as Brenda and I watched in expectation. All of a sudden, he reached into his pants pocket and removed a small knife, which he proceeded to stab into the wall facing us. Bits of plaster began to fall as everyone stood back watching this miserable attempt at demolition. Curiously, the owner observed the scene yet never raised her hand or voice to stop our actions, or even to ask why this man with a pocketknife was trying to knock down her wall. It was clear to all after less than a minute of Feri's feeble efforts that the wall would not be destroyed.

Although I would have been willing to continue the attempt for a much longer period, my mother said,

Listen, Han, it's no use. It's okay. I got vhat I came to see.

But, ma . . .

Han, listen, dere is noting else ve can do right now. Dat's it.

And so, still carrying my vision of holding my grandmother's wedding ring in my hand and taking it back to America, I deferred to my mother's decision and gave up my second goal of the day. We stepped outside and, eyeing a plum tree near the side entrance with low-hanging branches within our reach, we each grabbed a plum and ate the delicious fruit on the spot. It was a plum tree that had been planted by my grandmother in the 1930s, no doubt her contribution to the village production of *lekvar*, the thick, smooth plum jam used in many Hungarian recipes. The sweet taste of that plum, whose pit I wish I had saved, still lingers now as a remembrance of my grandmother's close kinship with nature. It was not the jewelry, but it was a close second.

Still reeling from Bela's bombshell that a distant cousin of my mother's had presumed to claim himself heir to the family's property, my mother boldly asked the owner to send her the deed. She wanted to see the facts in print, and the owner agreed to send it as soon as possible in return for the promise of American dollars. It was mailed so quickly that we received the deed in Miskolc just before leaving the country. It confirmed that the current owner had, indeed, purchased the property from my mother's cousin, but at that point the heat of the moment had passed and not much attention was paid to the document.

My mother did not seem concerned about whether she had rightful ownership to the property anymore. Having seen it once again, she seemed to have no further interest in it. The deed was put aside and never looked at again. To this day, I do not know what my mother did with it. But I know that she wrote to the owner a few months after our departure, admitting our mission, and received the following reply:

March 12, 1984

Dear Szidike and daughter and family —
I received your kind letter and I understood that you received the deed I promised and was in a hurry to send. Sorry to remind you, but you promised $100 that I expect as I need it. My husband is still ill and in the hospital, and our life is not easy.

Dear Szidi, please forget your secret that you were looking for because the wall was demolished in 1947. I examined the area, and I am sure it is not as it was when you left it. I feel sorry about that, because if it had not been demolished, I assure you, I could have searched and returned it intact. It seems as though someone might have been lucky in 1947, but I don't know who it could have been. It wasn't us because the deed shows that we didn't buy the property until later. I asked around, but nobody knows about it. Once again, I'm sorry. But anyway, dear Szidike, if you come back to Dámóc, I will gladly welcome you and your family at our place, and we could spend time and chat.

I told my husband about you, and he remembers you when he was eight years old. I will send a few embroidered things for your daughter, but now I am very busy working to support us. Dear Szidike, please write, and believe everything I have said and try to stay calm.

Many greetings and kisses to your whole family.

Mariska

As far as I know, my mother never sent the $100 nor responded to this letter, willing to let the whole matter rest, and I went along with her wishes.

In Dámóc that day, the village residents remained lined up in the street awaiting our emergence from the house. Some were singing and dancing in the middle of the road, and others had brought wine, seltzer, and fruit in celebration of someone who lived in their town a long time ago. The people seemed to be from my mother's generation, their children having gone to the bigger cities to find work. As we walked among the gathered residents, my mother recognized their faces and remembered their names, and there was an easy exchange of memories and anecdotes from the days when my mother's family had lived among them. A look of astonishment and then tears moistened the face of one man when my mother expressed her sympathy, recalling a tragic incident when a rearing horse accidentally killed his five-year-old son. I could see both laughter and tears on the faces of many of those who waited to talk to her.

Sidonia, Feri, and the author stand amid a group of villagers, Dámóc

My Hungarian conversation that day was limited to the two Hungarian phrases I had practiced studiously before we left for our trip. I repeated the first one over and over to each of the village residents as we were introduced, *Nagyon örülök hogy látom,* Very nice to see you. *Nagyon örülök hogy látom.* Fearful that the villagers would think I was a fluent Hungarian speaker and therefore initiate conversation, I was relieved that most of them did not, probably recognizing my shamelessly crude accent.

As my mother and the village residents interacted, I was struck by the contrast in clothing between my mother, dressed in a pair of white cotton jersey slacks with a bright multicolored, print-patterned blouse, and the women in the village, dressed in dark, ill-fitting housedresses and kerchiefs. My mother had become full figured since middle age, wore circular brown-rimmed glasses, and sported short, wavy gray hair, still with streaks of the dark brown color it once had been. Her self-made clothes were indeed flattering to her frame. I tried to imagine what she would have looked like had she remained in this setting. Would she also have worn a loose-fitting housedress with kerchief, lacking any modern style or sophistication? I found it impossible to picture her any other way than how she looked that day.

Then, my mother stopped to talk to a short, balding, shirtless man, who looked roughly her age and seemed to know her well. They enjoyed a lively discussion, of which I understood nothing, that is, until he began to name, one by one, each of the members of my mother's family in the form of a question. After each name, my mother shook her head from side to side, meaning no, and the man concurrently shook his head in disbelief, a look of deep sorrow crossing his face. Looking over my mother's shoulder, I immediately understood the questions he asked. *Tell me, did your father Simon survive? What about Dezso, Szeren, Etel, and Laura?* That conversation, consisting in large part of gestures only, was the first time I had ever heard anyone other than my mother utter those names. Lacking any photos of this lost family, these names, spoken by a complete stranger, meant more to me than anything else I saw in Dámóc. It was true. I had proof. They were real: Simon, Dezso, Szeren, Etel, Laura, and my mother had lived here, remembered well by their neighbors.

I realized then how my mother and her family were unable to recognize the bias inherent in that tiny hamlet tucked away near the northeast border of Hungary. I did not doubt the sincerity of these villagers when they expressed their excitement about the return of a long lost member of their community, or the sorrow exhibited by the man who discovered the fate of individual members of the Perlstein family. Yet, it had been a neighbor across the street who had consented to escort the Jews out of Dámóc in his horse and wagon to their eventual fate. Why was there no attempt to hide the few Jews who lived there? And the treasured family jewels hidden in the hearth in 1944 — who had them now?

My mother never shared the conflicted emotions I had about her home village. She remembered these people as good friends. If she ever had doubts or disappointment, she had stowed them in her unconscious and had refused to allow them to the surface. These were the residents among whom she had played and lived as a child and young adult. She still held memories of how they had all worked together as a community, each playing their part in maintaining its economic and social vibrancy. She could not, or would not, remember the betrayal and indifference of her last days there, possessing not even one ounce of vengefulness or anger toward them. Not like me.

We left Dámóc after visiting several more of the residents' homes, including my mother's Uncle Shayme's former house, the biggest one in Dámóc, and the location for Jewish communal prayer services in my mother's day, since the town was too small to have its own synagogue. As we were about to reenter our car, I pronounced the second Hungarian phrase I had learned, although I had planned to reserve it until our departure from our Hungarian cousins who had hosted us throughout our trip. Instead, I found myself saying it to the villagers: *Viszontlátásra,* See you again. *Viszontlátásra,* I kept repeating, declaring it as though somehow this would not be my last visit.

This time, we decided to take a different route back to Miskolc by way of Sátoraljaújhely, the nearby former capital city of the region, at the base of the Sator Hills near the foot of the Carpathian

Mountains. My mother had visited this city many times in her youth, and it had been the location of the nearest Jewish ghetto in northeast Hungary during World War II. In the car, my mother reached into her purse to pull out a boxed Timex watch that she had brought with her from America.

I asked whom the watch was for, and she responded, *It's for Kis Etu* [Little Etu].

What do you mean, it's for Kis Etu? What makes you think she is in Sátoraljaújhely? I asked, recalling her mentioning the name a number of times in the past.

I not sure, Han. I just hear she could still be in da town, she replied, looking away from me and out the window. At the time, I did not ask how she might have known this, just as I could not bring myself to ask about so many things. I just went along with my mother's intuition.

As we drove into Sátoraljaújhely, one of the first buildings we saw was a Jewish synagogue, tucked behind a thick iron gate. We stepped out of the car to see whether we could gain entrance, but the gate was locked and the edifice looked dark, lifeless, and abandoned. I imagined it in a former time, when congregants filled it for celebrations of the Sabbath, Jewish holidays, and other joyous family occasions like weddings and bar mitzvahs. It was obvious that this synagogue had been plagued by neglect and disuse for a very long time.

We started to walk down the street near the synagogue, wondering how to find someone to talk to about this house of prayer and also to ask about Little Etu. We all agreed that a direct approach was best. Stopping the first person we encountered on the street, my mother asked the man, *Excuse me sir, can you tell us where to find a Jew?* The man pointed with his index finger across the street, *If you cross this street and open the gate over there, you'll see an apartment building. Look for apartment 3A, and you'll find a Jew.*

We introduced ourselves to the older couple in apartment 3A, and they cordially invited us inside. They explained that they had returned after the war, but by then the city had lost most of its Jewish population, and in the intervening years, those who remained had either died or relocated. There were not ten Jewish men, the number required by the Orthodox tradition to conduct a prayer service, and certainly not enough to keep open the synagogue we had found.

Also, by the way, you are not the only visitors we have seen from America in the past two weeks, they remarked. *Two men also visited Dámóc to pay their respects to their grandmother's grave, and later they stopped here to pay us a visit.* We all looked at one another, understanding that the two candles on my grandfather's sister's grave had been lighted by those two men, cousins we had never met.

My mother then asked whether the couple knew Little Etu, offering her full name, but they replied that they knew all the Jews in the city, and Etu was not among them. My mother showed little emotion, but I saw her clutch the watch's box in her purse. In 1983, I did not understand the significance of this moment for my mother, and she could not tell me. I wondered what would have made her think she would find someone she had not seen or heard from in forty years. Was there some compelling information about Kis Etu of which I was not aware? I wondered, but I never asked.

I could not understand her disappointment until 1998, when I read Little Etu's letter to my mother. I knew immediately that my mother had never responded to her pleas for information. She had been too ashamed to tell her "buddy" that she had given birth to a child out of wedlock, and in the intervening thirty-six years, there had been no communication between them. That letter, written from Sátoraljaújhely in 1947, formed the basis of my mother's hope that Little Etu would still be there and that the two friends would finally meet once again.

We returned home to New England, each with our own memories of our trip to Hungary: our journey through the northeastern countryside, my mother's family home, the elucidation of how my mother and her family were taken away, the little Jewish cemetery, the welcome from the residents of Dámóc, our stop in Sátoraljaújhely, and all the revelations it produced. But we did not have much discussion with each other about our experiences, except for our opinions about what could have happened to the jewelry. Whoever the owner was at the time, my mother and I were both convinced that the jewelry had been removed when the wall was built. Or, if not then, perhaps it was removed the same evening we left the village, everyone there knowing that we must have had a good reason to attempt demolition of the wall. We would never know the jewelry's ultimate fate.

A year later, in response to my mother's letter requesting their assistance in tending the little Jewish cemetery, the owners of the adjacent property wrote:

My dear Szidike and family,

I received your kind letter. Sorry for the delay in responding. We have both been sick lately, and my husband was in the hospital for two weeks, but we are back home now. We understand from your letter that you wish the graves to be put in good order. It will be done. My son Bela, who was the one who was home when you visited, will do it. We were happy to receive the pictures and will keep them always. I am lighting candles on the graves, and Berte is keeping them in order, and watering the plants in the hope of seeing you again.

With affectionate kisses from far away.

The Hajdu family

We never visited Hungary again, though we talked about it a few times. As my mother aged, it seemed too taxing a trip, and I could not contemplate it without her. These days, I often think about a journey back to my mother's ancestral home near the foothills of the Carpathian Mountains. I want to find my grandmother's grave, and perhaps the jewels of my grandparents still await my claim.

21 Buttonholes

Buttonholes are basically slits cut through the fabric...most often horizontal, less often vertical; now and then, diagonal. . . . Have, first and foremost, a pair of good scissors with very sharp blades and points. Also a 6" ruler, a longer ruler or yardstick, and a contrast-colored pencil, not too hard and very sharp. — "Buttonholes," pages 32 and 33

At her barracks leader's repeated urging, my mother finally emerged from her barracks at Bergen Belsen to greet the liberating British forces. Emaciated, lice-ridden, and delirious, she barely realized the immensity of the occasion in which she was participating. She did not understand until later the revulsion exhibited by the British soldiers at the sight of the camp's depravity and the wretched souls they found within it, and she was not yet fully cognizant that she was alone in the world, the sole survivor of her family.

I couldn't tink about it, Hani. If I vould, I vouldn't be able to live, I remember her telling me once.

Soon after liberation, many of the survivors of Bergen Belsen were moved from the concentration camp to a former German army training camp about a mile and a half away, whereupon the British soldiers set the typhus-infested concentration camp ablaze to stop the spread of contagion. Within another month or so, my mother was moved again to the officer's quarters, where, she told me, the accommodations were a little more comfortable.

She spoke little about those years between 1945 and 1949 compared with the long narratives of her concentration camp experiences. I heard a few shadowy references to friends, a mention of goods purchased, such as dinnerware and candelabra, or the story of an occasional event, like a trip to the Nuremburg trials and a commemoration on the first anniversary of the liberation in 1946. Nothing about the Jewish committee that was created only three days after the liberation or the kindergarten, schools, hospital, cultural and religious activities, or political advocacy for Jewish emigration to Palestine.

She was never able to talk about how she felt as the lone survivor of her family, about life in the displaced persons camp, or about the circumstances of my birth. She did tell me that I was delivered by a Dr. Wycott, whom she described as a benevolent former Nazi doctor at Glyn Hughes Hospital, a facility named after the deputy director of medical services for the British Second Army and director of the relief operation that followed liberation. As usual, I never seemed to have the nerve to ask her more about these details, or any of the other things I longed to know. The pictures and letters I snatched from my mother's drawer in my 1998 nightstand theft, and the others that I found after her death, were my best clues to piecing together the story.

The sheer volume of photos that appeared to have been taken at the displaced persons camp was astounding. I poured over them, closely examining the array of portraits and scenes. Many of the pictures portray groups of young men and women appearing to be in their twenties and thirties apparently eager to have their pictures taken. They often posed in front of the stucco-and-brick dormitory buildings that served as their residences, or in the forest or heath area that surrounded them in Lower Saxony.

In a few snapshots they are sitting around a table, wine bottles and ashtrays cluttering its surface, or at a photographer's studio at various stages during that four-year period. If I had not known the time and place, I would have guessed they were graduate students on a college campus, enjoying one another's company. The fresh-faced smiles that looked at me as I gazed at these scenes attested to their spirit of rebirth and resilience just a short time after experiencing the worst terror and wretchedness they could ever have imagined.

Only one or two pictures have an inscription on the back to help me identify the individuals. One photograph shows a finely coiffed and dressed young man and woman, whose heads are leaning toward each other, bearing shy grins. He is wearing a pinstriped suit and a white shirt and tie, and she, a dark, shoulder-padded dress with a necklace peering out from the opening of her collar. I can barely make out the symbol inside the circle of the charm hanging from the thin chain, but it looks like the Hebrew letters Chet and Yod, together forming the word *Chai,* meaning "life." On the back of this two- by three-inch photo, the following inscription appears, written in Yiddish with a blue fountain pen:

June 6, 1947

As a remembrance, for my faithful sister, Perlstein Szidi, from me [sic] *your faithful brothers and good friend, Adler Eva and Richter Jozsi, Bergen Belsen Camp*

The signers of this message, putting their surnames first as is the European custom, bear the names of the few people my mother ever spoke of when parsing the meager details of this time. It is also one of the only pieces that I attempted to translate myself, given its short message and its transliterated letters. Written not in the Hebrew alphabet, which I would have found impossible, but using Roman letters, it is spelled in a way that probably conformed to the manner in which the writer pronounced Yiddish, with a distinct Germanic quality.

It strikes me as odd that the writer uses the first person singular when he or she writes "main getraie svester" (my faithful sister) and "fun mir" (from me), but then, in contrast, ends the sentence with a plural-singular combination, "der getraier brider und gute fraindin" (your faithful brothers and good friend). "Brider," the plural masculine word for 'brothers,' and the "me" and "my" at the beginning, leads me to believe that the inscription was written by the man, not the woman, who appears in the photo.

Jozsi, he vas a good friend my. He knew da girls who vere living mit me in my room at Bergen Belsen, an he introduce me to oder people. Ve vere togeder all da time, my mother told me assertively.

Did he speak Hungarian, ma? I asked when I first heard his name.

Yeh, ve all speak Hungarian un Yiddish.

Indeed, Jozsi's image appears many times in my mother's pictures from Bergen Belsen, confirming a strong bond between the two. Seeing the two faces in this photo also brought back my recollection that they were the people my mother and I had visited in Canada, later in 1952, on our first trip out of the United States after our arrival. On June 6, 1947, the date of the inscription, my mother was already more than six months pregnant. What did these two "faithful" friends know about her circumstances? How were they involved?

Moreover, who were the "we" of "ve all speak Hungarian" to whom she referred? Their identities were always clouded in a clutter of names around how they were related and where they came from in a constant, befuddling subterfuge so clever that I was never able to sort through the people and events of that time. It was as though she were so troubled by what had happened in the displaced persons camp, and in some ways even more so than by the atrocities of the concentration camps, that to reveal it would commit her to a life of shame and condemnation.

A few pictures reveal the reality of the setting. My mother, heavy set and grim faced, stands between two unidentified men beside an open crematorium, which appears to be on display. Several other pictures, probably taken on the same day, depict the unveiling of the 1946 memorial in honor of those who had perished at the original site of the Bergen Belsen concentration camp. The Jewish police are pictured marching in formation toward the memorial with their rifles and bayonets over their shoulders and then standing guard around the perimeter of the stone column on which is written, in Hebrew and English on opposite sides:

> *Israel and the World Shall Remember the Thirty Thousand Jews Exterminated in the Concentration Camp of Bergen Belsen at the Hands of the Murderous Nazis, Earth Conceal Not the Blood Shed on Thee! First Anniversary of Liberation, 15ᵗʰ April 1946 (14th Nissan 5706), Central Jewish Committee, British Zone.*

Perhaps this refers to the prophet Isaiah 26:21: "See, the Lord is coming out of his dwelling to punish the people of the earth for their sins. The earth will disclose the blood shed upon her; she will conceal her slain no longer."

I was drawn to one particular photo of a dashing police officer standing at ease at the base of the monument, his rifle vertical by his side. His face seemed to be everywhere among the mound of pictures, though sometimes he looked different, and I could not be sure I was seeing the same person.

Sidonia stands in front of the Hebrew side of the Bergen Belsen monument, probably in April 1946

Two other photos, one showing him in profile, and the other, facing front, were apparently taken at the same time at a photographer's studio. He appears very young, with a mischievous adolescent-like grin and thick dark hair, styled in a pompadour slicked back from his forehead. He is dressed in a casual sports jacket and open white collar at the neck, similar to the informal style adopted by the founders of the State of Israel that I had seen in magazines when I was younger.

Some pictures show him a little older, posing with a friend or relative, garbed in a more formal suit and tie, or sometimes a pea coat, his hair still piled high on his head, enhancing his tall, lean appearance. And a little older still, he stands in the back row, smiling among a dozen men with fedora hats surrounding a table covered with silver candleholders, cookies, and wine bottles, as though at the end of a Shabbat meal.

Finally, I looked again at the face on the familiar Jewish New Year card celebrating the Hebrew year 5708. The holiday that year began on the evening of September 14, 1947, sixteen days after my birth. I knew it was the same man I had seen in all the other photos, only a little more mature, his face more slender and angular, his full smile revealing a slight gap between his two top front teeth. He sits slightly sideways, but his face is turned to meet the camera lens. I recognized my own face in his. It confirmed what I had sensed since I was an adolescent and had glanced at the picture for the first time in my mother's drawer. He was my father.

What had our relationship been at that time? By the time these images came into my possession, I had spoken to him only once. On a sunny June morning in 1993, at 11:30 a.m., 6:30 p.m. Israeli time, with my heart pounding so loudly that I could hear it through my ears, I dialed what I had learned was my father's phone number. The following conversation occurred:

Hello, is Shmule there? I asked the woman who answered the phone.

He is on the porch, I'll get him, she responded, trying to muffle the mouthpiece with her hand, telling the man on the porch that a woman was calling asking for *Shmule.* Her extended vowel pronunciation of "Shmule," which sounded like "Shmuuule," indicated that perhaps he had not used that Yiddish version of his name in a long time. I heard a man's voice say hello quizzically.

Hello, this is Hanna, Szidi's daughter, I said, careful not to call myself *his* daughter.

Oh, how is your mother? he replied, his voice calm. If he had an accent, and I am sure he did, I paid no attention to it.

She's fine, getting older.

Well, we are all getting older.

How do you like it in Israel? I asked.

It's the only place a Jew should live, he commented with conviction.

After a short pause, I stated my purpose. *You're probably very surprised to hear from me after all these years, but I obtained your phone number, and I thought I would call you and see whether we could get together or be in touch in some way.*

Where do you live? he asked.

I live in the U.S.A., in Connecticut, actually. I have two children and work as a department head for a town in Connecticut.

Then he lowered his voice and spoke in a way that sounded as though his lips were resting directly on the mouthpiece of the phone. *You know, it's tough. It's very tough because nobody here knows about you*, he whispered.

You mean you've never told anybody? I asked incredulously, sensing that this man, whose voice had turned fearful from its previously composed tone, was concerned about my intentions.

No, I never told anybody here about you, he repeated with the same hushed voice.

Then, I can see how difficult it might be for you, I said, faking sensitivity to his acknowledgement. *Well, I'll give you my address and phone number, and if you ever feel like writing or calling, I'd love to hear from you.*

He paused as though writing down the information as I spelled my name and address and gave him my phone number.

Well, goodbye, I said, perceiving that the conversation had come to a close and there was nothing else I could say, *I'm glad we had this chance to talk.*

Yes, goodbye.

And that, with all my questions left unasked, was the first and last conversation I ever had with my father — not as hard as I thought, but painfully sharp.

22 Cutting

Cutting, with its irrevocable aspect — there's no denying that a mistake in cutting cannot be ripped out like a wrong seam — often makes a person nervous, especially if the fabric is expensive. — "Cutting," page 50

The more I looked at these pictures of people and scenes just after the war, the more I gleaned from the faces and settings they depicted. It is remarkable how the ninth and tenth viewings of the same photograph can elicit little details — the subtleties of a smile, a touch, a gesture — that enhanced my understanding of the story it told. The pictures of my mother, for example, show first a young, wide-eyed, full-cheeked, tentative woman posing for her picture in a photographer's studio soon after her settlement at the Bergen Belsen displaced persons camp. Four years later, she became a sullen, high-cheek-boned, resolute woman with trance-like eyes posing for her exit-visa photo. It is hard to believe they are the same person.

In one picture, she stood alongside two girlfriends on the street near some of the residences at Bergen Belsen. The two girls are dressed in knee-length skirts with knit sweaters, bobby socks, and what appear to be black oxford shoes. My mother, who became heavyset soon after her liberation, her body perhaps adjusting to a more normal diet, was taller than the others but dressed similarly, yet she is wearing stockings and black-strapped Mary Jane shoes. The photograph, probably taken early in her stay at Bergen Belsen, is so tiny that it's difficult to recognize the face, but her stance, the heels of her thick legs forming a right triangle as in an L-shape, much like a model's bearing, makes it irrefutably her image. She seems to be a part of this threesome, yet stands apart, not arm in arm as the other two.

Then there was that picture showing her standing between two men beside a crematorium that may have been on display at the commemoration of the first anniversary of liberation in April of 1946. Her face is sober, her bearing defiant. Looking straight at the camera, she shows more than a hint of the proud, stern woman I remember. The rest of the pictures of this era were taken between 1947 and 1949, beginning from just a few months after my birth to the time of our visa photos. It was during that period when the most profound changes in her visage occurred.

Sidonia stands between two unidentified men beside a crematorium on display, Bergen Belsen, probably April 1946

I was fascinated by several pictures that I had briefly seen as a youth when, like all children, I was captivated by seeing myself as a baby and toddler. When I look at the pictures that show my mother and me together, I notice that she is smiling. In any other photograph of this time, she appears stiff and solemn, but when she is with me, she seems instinctively to reveal her teeth in a tranquil smile.

The first set of photographs appears to have been taken when I was three or four months old. My mother, wearing a striped knit pullover with a matching cardigan, is holding me in her arms. She has already thinned out quite a bit from the earlier photos, her shaped cheekbones now noticeable, her dark hair swept up at the top and grown to shoulder length. I am dressed in a white knit jumpsuit and knitted bonnet, looking quizzically up at the photographer. My startled look seems to have caused my mother to gaze at me with a proud smile on her face, as though saying to the photographer: *See I have my whole world in my arms now.*

Sidonia holds her beloved child in her arms, Bergen Belsen displaced persons camp, 1947

A favorite photo location appears to have been the Lüneburg Heath, the site of the Bergen Belsen camp. The low-growing vegetation and dry patches of grass and soil marked with occasional footpaths can be clearly seen in a number of photographs taken in both warm and colder months. In one, my mother is holding me in her arms when I am about a year old. I can tell by the short-sleeved tops we are wearing that it is a warm season. As the sides of our heads barely touch in a whispering caress, my mother holds me in a way that simulates someone displaying a delicate piece of china, her hands cupped so gently underneath my bottom, it seems as though I am partially suspended in air. Her soft smile is so serene and her face so beautiful that, when I finally had the photograph in my possession in 1998, I stared at it for a long time. And I have done so many times since.

Sidonia delicately holding the author at about age one, Bergen Belsen, 1948

My fixation on this photograph, combined with the little I knew or had learned from other photos and letters, led me to fantasize about how this woman, my mother, came to have a child with the handsome young man, my father, whom I had seen in the many pictures that were part of her collection. It was a fantasy I never would have bothered to envision in my youth. I imagined the scene could have happened this way:

When my mother was liberated from the Bergen Belsen concentration camp, the family she knew and had clung to for reassurance and solace was gone. The life she had led in that small Hungarian village was over. She found herself among strangers who themselves had endured equally horrific circumstances. Although she was already in her thirties, she was a virgin in every sense of the word, isolated from men by her orthodox religious upbringing, which expected her to marry only when the right person of similar religious background could be located.

At the displaced persons camp, a group of young men whose homelands were in the expansive region of Europe once governed by the vanquished Austro-Hungarian Empire — all Hungarian speakers — lived either in or near my mother's residence. They dressed neatly in suits and ties, hair slicked back or sometimes covered with fedora hats, with handsome smiles on their faces. My mother's roommates perhaps knew these men from before the war and made introductions freely among the group. Or it might have been her "faithful" friend Jozsi, the man whose picture I had seen with Eva and in several snapshots, who introduced her to the man with whom she would enter into a romantic relationship.

He must have been boyish and charming to women. One friend of my mother's — whom we had met at Camp Wentorf and then saw a few times through the years when she, her husband, and her son were assigned to Worcester, Massachusetts — said to me recently that she remembered "a group of young men, one more handsome than the next, who went around Bergen Belsen in a bunch. I think that tall, skinny kid might have been your father." It seems to me that if that "tall, skinny kid" had exhibited any affection toward my mother at that stage of her life, she would have fallen easily for his advances.

I imagined my mother then at her most vulnerable, needing loving arms and a tender kiss — something to help her forget the constant ache in the pit of her stomach at having lost everything she had held dear. She needed someone to love her, to tell her that despite everything that had happened, it would turn out all right, to hold her and give her comfort. If that tall, skinny kid offered those promises, I can see her accepting.

Perhaps they stayed together for a while at Bergen Belsen, both finding consolation in each other. But then my mother learned she was pregnant. She decided to have the child and hoped the man would ultimately marry her, since having a child outside marriage was unheard of by both religious and cultural tradition. Yet, marriage seemed not to be a part of this equation. As I read in the following pencil-written letter, by the beginning of 1948, just a few months after my birth, discussion about my welfare ensued:

1952

Dear Chief Rabbi —
I am sorry to disturb you. I would like to introduce myself. My name is Perlstein Szidonia, and from 1944 to 1949, I was in Bergen Belsen, Block L2. In January 1948, I had a meeting in your apartment with Yungman Samuel. The basis of discussion was your legalization of my daughter with him, and the financial support from him, but we could not finish our negotiations in those troubled times.
Since then, four years have passed, and Yungman Samuel and I and my little daughter moved to America. I moved to Springfield, Massachusetts, thanks to the JOINT, and I recently learned that he is living in another state. The local committee is helping me with all their forces to legalize my daughter, and I am working hard, but I would like to receive some support from him. I would like to ask for your help to verify that a discussion occurred in January 1948 in your apartment when Yungman Samuel accepted the fact that he is the father of the child, and although he did not want to legalize her, he was willing to pay child support, and he declared in the presence of the chief rabbi that if I wished, he would pay in German currency the equivalent of sixteen years in one lump sum. As I did not wish to accept that offer, the case has been unsettled since 1948. My humble request from you is in some form to verify the fact of the negotiations and their content

where you were present. This letter would be a document for me in a legalization procedure.

I ask you to do as you see fit, and I am sorry to write in Hungarian, as I cannot write in Yiddish, only read, but you can respond in Yiddish. Thank you in advance, and I am sorry for disturbing you.

Perlstein Szidonia

When I read this letter, I wondered why a document that had purportedly been written by my mother and intended for the "chief rabbi" was still in her stash of letters. If she had written it, why had it not been mailed to the recipient? Also, the sophistication of the language and the penmanship used in the letter appears to be above her writing ability. The letter was most likely written by someone at the Springfield Jewish Social Services Bureau, which was the agency that assisted Jewish refugees with social and economic support and was referred to as the *local committee* in the letter. My mother had started working at the Victoria Dress Corporation only a year before this letter was written, and the agency was attempting to gain further economic assistance for her from the father of her child. My mother gave them the facts, and they must have arranged for the letter to be written in Hungarian.

I could only come to two conclusions regarding why this penciled letter still remained in the massive pile of correspondence, the only one supposedly written by my mother: Either the letter had never been mailed or this was just a draft of a letter that was later typewritten or inked in pen and mailed to the intended recipient. I never discovered the answer, never knew whether the chief rabbi had received this letter and responded, and, if he did, whether events occurred that helped my mother in her legalization attempt. She would never have confided any of that information to me, because to do so, she would have had to tell me about my father. That was something she could not do, except on one occasion.

Just a few months before my mother's move to elderly housing, I asked whether I could interview her on film about her life. She had refused to record or film any such recollection on numerous occasions in the past, so I expected nothing more than an emphatic negative reply yet again. But, to my surprise, she consented to sit for a dialogue with me. She was just about to turn eighty-five years old and perhaps felt that at least once before she died, she should reveal some of the details of her life for posterity.

I decided that the best way to elicit honest information from her was to hide behind the video camera so she could not see my face. She had never been able to look at me when relating sorrowful past events in her life. I bet myself that if she could not see me, she would be more at ease. Therefore, I set the camera on a tripod and tried to veil much of my presence in back of it so she would only hear my voice, as though it were detached from my body. To a certain extent, this maneuver worked. Although she often hesitated, changed the subject, made countless hand gestures, shifted her body, looked down at the floor, pointed out the growing darkness outside as daylight slipped away, and sometimes just could not remember some things, she recounted more of the facets of her painful history than ever before.

I began by asking her questions about her childhood and her Holocaust experiences. As she became tired, I ended with questions about her life in a displaced persons camp. In the end, that first interview was the only interview, since our pledges to continue where we had left off at a later date never came to fruition. Often, her account repeated many of the stories I had heard growing up, but as the video camera continued to roll, and as I became emboldened with my questions in my behind-the-tripod hideaway, I braced myself for any new kernels of information, determined to learn more about her life, and in turn, understand more of my own. The kernels came my way in several areas. At one point in the interview I asked:

> *Tell me again, ma, who was at home in Dámóc when you left that morning for the ghetto?*
>
> *It vas me, my fader, Laura, Szeren, and little Mordcha.*
>
> *Did you say that your sister Szeren was there with you?* (I asked this having heard about it before, but all of a sudden I wondered why Szeren would have been with her family after she had married and moved away.)
>
> *Vell, you know, she separated from da husband in Kisvarda. You know.* (She said this matter-of-factly, as though she had told me this in a previous conversation.)

This piece of information, conveyed in such a perfunctory tone, somehow startled me, and not only because I had not known it before. As I thought about it, I conjectured that her oldest sister's marital separation and reversion to a life independent of her husband may have provided a model for my mother in some way. The sister she had admired and respected the most had separated from her husband when convention frowned upon such action and was free to live life on her own terms. It was Szeren's presence of mind that night in the family home that led to the hiding of the family's precious jewelry. Later in the interview, I asked this question:

> *So, how did you come to have a baby in Bergen Belsen?*
>
> *I even don't know myself. It just happened,* she said, ostensibly in earnest.
>
> *It just happened?*
>
> *Yeh, it just happened, and I don't care,* she added, as though snubbing her nose at the air.

Then, sensing that I was getting close to an as-yet-unrevealed portion of her soul, she began, in her sly method of interjecting extraneous information, to turn to the subject of other people she had known in Bergen Belsen — a woman who spoke Hungarian, had a Polish husband and two kids, and who went to New York, and then someone else who went to Israel . . .

So you didn't care, ma? I asked in an attempt to get her back on point.

Vell, dat's vhy I vas mad on Jozsi.

You were mad at Jozsi?

Yeh, but ve vas close friends. I vas mad because he intro-duce me to . . . She trailed off, as though hesitating about what to say next.

He introduced you to my father, I said, saying those two words to her for the first time since I was six: "my father."

And then later you learned that you were pregnant?

Vell, I never knew dat I was pregnant, dat vas number von. She said this, though never having told me what number two in this train of thought was.

What did you think when you finally learned you were pregnant? I asked.

I blamed myself. I vas always on my two feet, and den I couldn't.

I took this to mean that she had always prided herself on keeping her wits and staying strong in her youth and during her later cata-strophic experiences. Once she became pregnant, she felt she had lost control over her life. I felt a wave of sympathy well up inside me upon hearing her say this, as though the baby were someone other than me.

I talk to a rabbi at da camp from Ujhel [Sátoraljaújhely] *about my situation and he talk to him, but it doesn't vork out, and after, I don't care,* she offered, saying it yet again, as though at that point she had regained her emotional strength and was saying it to the world.

So it was after this period of "I don't care" that my mother completed her stay at Bergen Belsen and decided to come to America with her little daughter. She was two women by then, the one who instinctively smiled whenever she held her child, and the one who posed for a sober, chilling visa photo with her chin held high, daring the photographer, or anyone, to tangle with her.

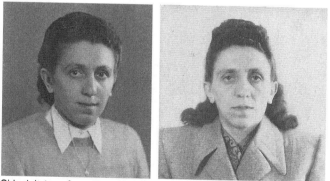

Sidonia's transformation, 1945 to 1949

23 Fitting

> Fitting a garment while sewing it should be a very small operation, involving small changes, the real alterations (if any) having been made in the pattern. . . . As a rule, however, fitting is done when all seams are stitched except side seams, waistline, and armhole seams, which should be basted. This will give you the total picture. — "Fitting a Garment," page 89

I think my mother knew my marriage was over before I did. By the end of the 1980s, that unspoken quality of our relationship, an implicit exchange of facial expressions, a downcast glance of our eyes, a purse of the lips, grew ever more telling that she and I were about to face yet another significant crossroads in our lives.

My marriage was crumbling after twenty years, a result of complex circumstances that could probably be reduced to the following simple explanation: I was seeking a father figure, and he, a mother figure, having lost his mother due to illness when he was only six. Neither one of us fit what the other wanted. Although at the time I could have pointed to a series of events over a period of years that provoked the breakup, the bottom line was that each of us sought to satisfy a primitive need for a parental presence we had been deprived of as children. It led to disappointment, disillusionment, rancor, and ultimately, to divorce in 1990, when my children were sixteen and ten years old.

No one was more devastated by the divorce than my mother. Her daughter and the man she had referred to as her own son would now lead separate lives. The family she treasured more than anything else in the world would be torn apart. For the next few years, she seemed to combine hatred for my former husband with a sense of confusion, loss, and shame.

> *I not gonna tell anyvon in Springfield dat you divorced, Han,* she advised me.
>
> *It's okay, ma. You can tell people. It's nothing to be ashamed about. The marriage just didn't work out. It happens.*
>
> *You mean you gonna tell everybody?*
>
> *I'm not going to tell everybody, but it's just really hard to keep something like that a secret for very long. Everybody's going to find out anyway.*
>
> *I don't care. I not gonna say anyting.*

Since Springfield, Massachusetts, is not too distant from Vernon, Connecticut, and the gossip grapevine has far-reaching tendrils, the news about my divorce did not take long to find some of my mother's acquaintances. Reluctantly, she gave in to acknowledging the truth. I did not feel as ashamed as she did about the dissolution of my marriage. Perhaps for her, it reignited the feelings of guilt and humiliation over her own failed relationship.

For me, the saddest part of my divorce had to do with "fit," by which I mean the fit of human belonging. My mother and I had spent our lives together hoping to find a group or a family with whom we could feel comfort and support, a group that would welcome us and truly love us, a group with whom we would fit. Although we never spoke of it, we each retained memories we wished not to repeat, like the lonesome Passover seders when my mother and I sat by ourselves almost every year reading our Maxwell House Haggadahs (after all, the ritual requires only a leader and a child) and eating a sumptuous meal cooked as though we had multiple family members at our table. We longed for those other seats to be filled.

The years of my marriage brought the first time I had ever been part of a two-parent nuclear family. Combined with my husband's extended relatives, it felt whole. With the divorce, my mother and I lost many of those ties, except with my two children, Brenda and Stephen, who continued to exhibit their nonjudgmental love despite the devastation of their parents' breakup. It was with those two young people, the children who reminded my mother of members of her lost family, that we secured the most permanent fit.

Yet, as I continued to read the documents in the pile of my mother's old correspondence, I found this curious letter, written in Hungarian in the mid 1950s, by the only other Perlstein from Dámóc who had survived the Holocaust:

My dear Szidike,

I do not even know how to begin. I don't remember the last time I held a pen. I received your letter two weeks ago, and I cannot tell you how many times I read each of its words. It reminded me of our old home. My children ask me what kind of letter this is that I read it so many times.

There isn't anything special I can write to you. Thank God we are well. My two boys are nine and a half and eight years old. They are very smart and study in Yiddish, as well as English, which is a little bit harder for them because they cannot speak it. My husband makes a living, and I also worked earlier this year, but now there is no work. Come and visit us one day.

My dear Szidike, with today's mail I received the letter that requires my signature, but I cannot sign because my husband's name is written on it. I do not know what you filed there. I am surprised that you do not know my name.

I am registered under the name Rosalia, just like at home. Write to me and let me know what I should do with it.

I end this letter here because the pen is shaking in my hand. I kiss you many times.

Chaje Szore and family
Dear Chanele, I kiss many times separately.

The tone of this correspondence surprised me. Just as the writer reread the letter my mother had written to her, I read this letter over and over again, trying to make sense of its contents. My mother had mentioned this cousin various times in my childhood, referring to her as Zali, her first cousin, whose mother was my grandfather's sister, also a resident of Dámóc along with her husband and family. When I asked why we had never met this cousin, my mother replied in her distinct cryptic manner:

Vell, Hani, dis cousin don't vant to see me.
Why wouldn't she want to see you, ma?
I not sure. I just remember in da Bergen Belsen DP camp, ve see each oder, and she vas mad on me.
Why?
Who knows? She say I should vear a sheitel, and I don't vant to.

I took my mother's word for this and thought that Zali was angry with her. I had always thought that there was no use in calling Zali or in writing to her.

As I read this stunning letter many years later, I imagined that my mother's shame at producing a child out of wedlock must have led to her confusion, if that is what it was, about how she fit with this remaining cousin and Jewish society in general. If her cousin had, indeed, made a comment about my mother's not wearing the head covering worn by religious married orthodox Jewish women to reflect their modesty, my mother may have construed it as disapproving of her status as a single mother and projected her own self-condemnation onto Zali.

I surmised that the letter was most likely in response to a request for a signature on an affidavit relating to a restitution case my mother had initiated with the German government — "I don't know what you filed there." This cousin would have been the only one still alive who could have attested to daily contact with my mother in that remote village. She was the only one who could, in turn, provide evidence about my mother's earlier life, to help in determining the effects of the Holocaust on my mother's psychological and physical condition. This kind of information was valuable in supporting my mother's application for restitution.

My mother was willing to ask the cousin for a signature but could not face Zali in person. There was the paradox. So, despite this letter's tender and heartfelt words, my mother had rejected her cousin's plea to "come and visit one day," deciding that she no longer fit into the world to which her cousin belonged. It turned out that it was Zali's two sons, who were "nine and a half and eight years old" when my mother received that letter, who, almost thirty years later, preceded us by two weeks to the Dámóc Jewish cemetery to light candles on their grandmother's grave.

My understanding of the search for fit rose fully to my consciousness in 1992, when I decided to try again to secure restitution from the German government for the psychological trauma my mother had experienced as a result of the horrors she witnessed during the Holocaust. We made many attempts at establishing a case for her, dating back to 1955, hence the crucial letter to her cousin. Yet, aside from small amounts of reimbursement for medical bills and a token few hundred dollars as *Wiedergutmachung* ('reparation' or 'compensation'), we were not successful in convincing the German courts of the validity of my mother's claim.

I brought my mother to Dr. Dori Laub, a psychoanalyst in New Haven, Connecticut, himself a child survivor of the Holocaust, to ask his assistance in ascertaining her deep psychological suffering. It was during the second session with him, where I was present, that I heard my mother pronounce the most revealing admission of her feelings.

> *So you lost your sister Laura at Bergen Belsen?* Dr. Laub asked.
>
> *Yes, she vas very sick, so I bring her to da camp hospital von night*, she responded, looking straight ahead, pretending I was not in the room.
>
> *And then what occurred?*
>
> *I come back in da morning and I ask for her, and dey say she is outside. I look outside and all I see is a pile of dead people*, she replied, her hands gesturing in the form of a mound, her face sullen.
>
> *Did you feel some guilt then about what happened to your sister?* he asked, perhaps sensing that she held some profoundly conflicted emotions about this.
>
> *Guilt, I don't know about guilt, but if she live, den I vould have somebody.*

With this sentence, "den I vould have somebody," I gained more insight into my mother's true feelings than I ever had before.

I was not offended by her statement. I understood that a child is not the same as a sister, someone closer to your own age, with whom you can share secrets and ask advice. Had Laura lived, my mother's life would have been much different. I am certain of that. Here was the first expression of her aloneness of almost fifty years.

I have relived this scene and that assertion in my head many times since I first witnessed her saying it. Her words drew me close to her. Of course, I was also struck by her different version of Laura's death than the one I had heard when I was younger. My mother had always claimed that her sister had died in her arms, a fantasy she preferred over the true version.

After a few sessions with Dr. Laub, we discontinued our original restitution efforts and applied instead for new hardship funds that had finally been offered by the German government to survivors to supplement their income. We never saw Dr. Laub again, but I know that if we had not met him, I might never have had these glimpses into my mother's subconscious. It was another small crack in her tough exterior that helped me along on my journey of self-revelation.

Over the next few years, as my mother continued to visit us every Sunday, she began to occasionally envision me as Laura.

Remember vhen ve vere in Dachau, and ve vere valking to da castle an you find your coat?

Yeah, and that woman just wouldn't believe our story about how it was our coat. I replied so swiftly that I surprised myself.

Do you remember vhat her face look like?

I knew that I could not respond to this question because I had not been there. I was forced to say, *Sorry, ma, I don't. I wasn't there.*

Oh, I'm sorry, Han, for a minute I tought you vere Laurie. Vhat's wrong mit me?

But I think the disappointment was more mine because I found that I was proud of my ability to banter with my mother in this way. Sometimes I wanted to be Laura, to be my mother's confidante, the sister who shared her memories of a past life, to be the Laura who was still alive, not dead in a heap of starved, diseased bodies.

On those Sundays, my children anticipated their grandmother's arrival with a combination of dread and excitement. They did not look forward to her obsessive need to barge into their rooms to clean them, throwing out anything she saw as junk, all the while referring to them as *mamele* and *tatele,* little mommy and daddy. Perhaps her compulsion to clean, which became more pronounced in her later years, was her subconscious way of keeping the world in order, to control her surroundings and mine, so that nothing could again disrupt her structured life. Later, we all rummaged the garbage pails to withdraw the items she had discarded. But, in her defense, she also taught them to fold their clothes, sort and wrap their coins, and look their best. She mended their socks and ripped seams, rewarded their academic achievement with crisp new dollar bills, and sewed new outfits for Brenda.

Then, every week we would go to my bedroom to change my sheets, pillowcases, and duvet covers, which she had made on her sewing machine from extra flat sheets sewn together, buttoned on one end. As we each started at either end, buttoning the duvet buttons, I never told her that I was racing her to see who could reach the middle faster. I never won, despite my concerted and repeated efforts.

We did not have much of a conversation on those Sundays, nor did we spend time sitting in the living room just to relax. She had to make herself useful. That was her job. That's how she perceived her fit in our family. As soon as she was finished, she had lunch and then drove herself back to Springfield to face her sewing jobs at home. She never made it easy for me to divulge my deepest thoughts to her.

That was why, after I had talked to my father on the phone that summer morning in 1993, I resolved never to tell her about it. I would not have known even how to approach her to reveal this most unanticipated and unsettling conversation. It was difficult to confide in her. On the other hand, I never kept important matters from her either. She had spent many years keeping the mystery of his identity sewn up inside. I knew that if I told her about the phone call, it would have created excruciating emotional pain, pain from which I wanted to shield her at all costs. From then on, mustering all my will, I kept my new discoveries about my mother's past to myself.

24 Thread and Needles

Thread and needle, without which no sewing could be done, are practically a unit. Not only is one useless without the other, but, to do a proper job, they must be suited to one another. And, above all, to the fabric you want them to stitch. — "Thread and Needles," page 164

When I hung up the phone after talking to my father on that day in June of 1993, I was confused about my emotions. It was not the kind of exchange I had expected. Contrary to my illusion about his eagerness to finally hear from his long lost daughter, he was cautionary, secretive, and fearful that he might be exposed for a mistake he had made many years ago. He did not seem interested in meeting me, the daughter he had left before the age of two, to see how I had turned out. Yet, I had a gnawing feeling that I needed to see him in order for me to be complete. If I could just meet him, even just once, it would be enough to sew up this raveled seam that I had carried with me for so long.

I followed the phone call with letters, but there was no response. Then, just a few months after our conversation, I received a phone call from his daughter, the product of his marriage in the 1950s, who also lived in Israel. She told me that after my call, my father broke down and told her and her mother about me. She wondered whether we could meet when she came to the States. On the two occasions we met, I observed that she looked a little like the image of the young man I had seen in my mother's photos, but that I more closely resembled that youthful, charismatic face. Would he not want to see the person who most reminded him of his own likeness?

I was single-minded: I wanted to meet my father. I thought my half-sister could facilitate that aim, and even when she advised me many times in the letters that followed that it would not be possible, I persisted. It sometimes felt as though I were disputing with a part of myself, both she and I the progeny of the same human creature. We were both intransigent and eventually, after a few years, she never contacted me again, probably worn down by my determined requests for her to pave the way for that face-to-face encounter. My window of opportunity seemed closed after that, but I still felt an urgency to see my father's face and to talk to him again, although I was not sure what I wanted to say or what he wanted to hear.

The meetings, the letters, and the angst all transpired without my mother's knowledge. Keeping this information from her, and the events that occurred later, set me on a path, not only of protecting her from painful truths, but also of separating myself from the threads that had bound us during my childhood and early adulthood.

I was a single parent then, and I began to date other men, ultimately landing in a long-term relationship with a quiet man eight years my senior. Steeped in his Catholic faith, patient yet stern, he was much as I imagined a father. I began to keep most of the details about my personal life private from my mother, instinctively feeling that she would not approve. She never advised me to end the connection with my new partner, nor did she directly voice her displeasure, but after years of nonverbal communication, I understood her look, her sigh, her mumbling under her breath. She did not like my relationship, though I continued it anyway.

Yet, with all my attempts at independence in the 1990s, many aspects of my life inextricably intertwined me with my mother. Through the years, we became identified as a duo, belonging together as though we were one. In addition to our successful creative partnership in which I continued to showcase her remarkable designs, we regularly ate at restaurants together, and she always paid the bill. We shopped for shoes, she a wide and I a narrow; we purchased patterns and fabric during our frequent excursions to Osgoods; and we worked together on the documents for her payment requests to the German government. Sometimes I would grab her checkbook and write the checks for some of her living expenses, dismayed at her distorted spelling of the names of her creditors: *AT–T Brodbend, Verizone, and Northiest Utilitis.*

Informed that the Hungarian government would finally compensate victims for property confiscated during World War II, my mother was asked to list the assets owned by the Perlstein family before its deportation. Of course, my mother considered the most important asset to be the house her family had built in the decade before its expulsion, the new home that had produced such joy and excitement among all her family members. The deed to the house (sent to us by the current owners, whom we met on our visit to Hungary) had been virtually ignored, placed somewhere never to be found again. Yet we knew that it showed a distant cousin had claimed the property and had later sold it to the current owners. Was there another document showing the original owners of the property to be the Perlsteins? We wrote to the Land Authority in Sátoraljaújhely to find out. In short order, it sent us our answer, the property title document, a translated excerpt of which follows:

Received 1939 January 7

Thereafter, the ownership right for the real estate is transferred from subdivision 322 to A.T.2 to the five persons list-

ed below, *residents of Dámóc, by the right of the wife of Mrs. Perlstein Simon, born Klein Hani as a compensation/exchange as an inheritance entitlement and in equal shares.*

Mrs. Frankfurt Herman, born Perlstein Szeren
Perlstein Etel
Perlstein Laura
Perlstein Dezso and
Perlstein Szidonia, residents of Damoc
To the benefit of the persons above.

The property title indicates that as a result of the death of my grandmother, Hani Klein Perlstein, the property was inherited by my mother and her siblings in equal shares. Later, in 1958, the distant cousin mentioned on our visit to Dámóc also claimed ownership as an inheritance. However, the last person of the "five persons" who legitimately held ownership, my mother, was still alive, calling into question his right to inherit. Under the circumstances, we felt we had a good chance for compensation.

Then there was the jewelry. Written on the cardboard insert of a package of nylon hosiery, my mother listed the following items of her family's jewelry, not in Hungarian or in English, but in clear, understandable German:

1 Gold Zigarettenetui: 1 gold cigarette case
1 Gold Armbanduhr: 1 gold wristwatch
1 p[aar] Gold Manschettenknoepfe, passender: 1 pair gold
   matching cufflinks
1 Gold Verlobungsring mit Brillant: 1 gold engagement
   ring with diamond
1 Krawattennadel mit Brillant: 1 tie tack with diamond
1 Gold Brosche: 1 gold brooch

324 szám B). Tulajdoni lap. *Dámóc*

Sorszám		Jegyzet
	[handwritten entry]	
1.	*Perlstein Sajma* dámóczi	B. 3.
2.	*[handwritten entry]*	
3.	*[handwritten entry]*	
4.	Frankfurt Hermanné szül. Perlstein Szerén	B.9.
5.	Perlstein Etel	B.9.
6.	Perlstein Laura	B.9.
7.	Perlstein Dezső és	B.9.
8.	Perlstein Szidonia, dámócki lakosok javára bekebeleztetik.	B.9.

The portion of the Dámóc land records citing the heirs to the Perlstein property, in 1939 being the five living offspring of Hani and Simon Perlstein

1 Gold Uhrkette: 1 gold watch chain
1 p[aar] Gold Ohrring mit Brillant: 1 pair gold earrings with diamonds
1 Platin Ring mit Brillant: 1 platinum ring with diamond
10 Golddollarstücke [Gold-Dollar Stücke]: 10 gold dollars
15 Goldrubelstücke [Gold-Rubel-Stücke]: 15 gold rubles

Upon reading her list, astounded at her proficient memory even into her eighties, I learned in more detail what we had missed on our trip to Hungary. Finally knowing the specific items left behind, I longed for them even more than that day we attempted to knock down the wall in a vain effort to release them from their hiding place. The Hungarian government's compensation for lost property: $125.

By the 1990s, I had acquired many of my mother's character traits, even though I swore in my youth, as many children do, that I would rather die than be like her. Just as she was reluctant to place her trust in others, perhaps for fear of betrayal, I found that I, too, was cautious about misplacing my trust, treating too many people with suspicion and wariness, often without justification. My mother had few close friends during her life in America, yet I was fortunate to connect with some who dared to peel away my layer of distrust and reserve to form long-term friendships.

I had also picked up a character trait that came from my mother's prideful manner, which I often observed in her. I had the tendency to overlook the nuances of events, including the conversations and behavior of others that may have been detrimental to my life. With my head up and facing forward, I sometimes missed the cues that may have been visible on the periphery. If I did notice them, I preferred to adhere to my mother's axiom about avoiding confrontation wherever possible. It often helped me to steer clear of truths that I should have squared up and faced, but instead addressed only when there was no other choice, like my divorce. I often thought my mother was pleased that I had adopted her distrustful and prideful nature as my own. In a way, that created a bond between us. We tacitly agreed to trust only in each other and no one else. It was part of what made my mother and me such a good pair.

On the other hand, she had also taught me to work hard, be frugal, not to let people take advantage of me, be humble, take solace from my accomplishments, and exude an air of confidence by standing straight, with my shoulders back (not always a sign of excessive pride). If I had any success in my work, I know it was because of those values that my mother had taught me.

Stephen's Bar Mitzvah, 1993. The author wears a home-made black crepe dress with sheer sleeves and gold lamé shawl, and Brenda wears a silk taffeta dress with lace blouson sleeves

My mother had long since put her bank accounts in my name, but she wanted to keep close tabs on the money she had saved from the moment she arrived in the United States, sometimes in two-dollar deposits. She kept track of the certificate of deposit expiration dates and the exact amounts, to the penny, of principal and accumulated interest like an obsessed fan keeping a stat sheet at a ball game. She never allowed any withdrawals and steadfastly refused to put her hard-earned dollars in another investment vehicle like the stock market, deciding it to be too risky. She wanted to be assured her money would never disappear. For my mother, a trip to the bank ranked as high as a trip to Disney World for most people.

She knew bank tellers by their first names and was fussy about which one she chose to handle her accounts. Often, I would accompany her on these bank trips, and our experience would unfold something like this:

Okay, ma, there's a bank teller's open window right there.

I don't vant to go dere.

Why not?

I vant to go to da lady at da desk.

It doesn't really make any difference which teller you go to, ma.

Yes, Han, it make a difference. Dat teller at da vindow don't know anyting.

Well, you don't know that, ma, but okay, we'll wait for the lady at the desk.

Good, because I have a zipper bag for her, she said, showing me one of the hundreds of patterned zippered cloth bags she had sewn.

After waiting a while, we finally sat down in the partitioned office of one of the bank managers. Carefully reviewing all the fine details of the status of the account, sometimes pointing out errors in the term or interest rate, she thanked the manager, offering her the handmade zippered bag.

Tank you so much for helping us, she said, as the manager invariably gushed at having received such a thoughtful, attractive gift. *Ve see you again next time!* Then, as soon as we walked out of the bank, she turned to me with a smug grin, *See, Han, now dat vas a good teller.* And so, all the tellers and bank managers, at least the female ones, at the banks in which she held her money, owned zippered cloth bags from a faithful customer.

My mother also became very opinionated during the last twenty years of her life, particularly about the way people dressed. Her nonconfrontational style gave her the appearance of someone who kept her judgments to herself, but when it came to fashion, her strong opinions prevailed.

Han, look on her dress, she would whisper in my ear but in an audible voice, eying someone at a wedding. *Shame on her for vearing such a shmate* [rag]. *It don't fit her at all.*

Concerned that her criticism might be heard by others, but particularly by the woman in question, I responded, *Ma, stop talking that way. It's not nice to say things like that in public.*

> *But, Hani, it's true. I just can't stand it. Maybe I should tell her.*
>
> *Ma, please, stop it! No! Sha!* I reprimanded through my teeth.
>
> *It's terrible*, she said, trilling the "rr" in "terrible" for emphasis.

I understand, ma, but you can't do anything about it.
You've got to stop.
Okay, but . . .
Sha, please!
Okay.

It was a scene that played out over and over, almost every time we went somewhere together. She could not tolerate fools or poor dressers. So we traded places: whereas she had been the one to say *Sha*, when I was a child, I assumed that role as an adult. I was embarrassed by her behavior, to be sure, but also found it amusing that she was so observant and adroit in her fashion assessments.

The 1990s ushered in the era of the little black skirt. As my mother grew older, she was not as prolific in producing the number of outfits she had turned out in the 1970s when I was working in Hartford. She viewed the simple, chic black skirt as the staple of any good wardrobe. It matched with almost every other color or pattern, assuming a ubiquitous role in creating an outfit. In her last two decades, my mother fashioned innumerable black skirts in a full range of fabrics, including wool, crepe, polished cotton, jersey knit, brushed cotton, polyester, linen, and silk. They were all straight skirts, comfortable yet slimming and fitted to the body, with four darts in the front and back and a slit vent in the back. Sometimes, if she was low on fabric, there was a seam in the center front as well as at the back and sides.

The one-and-one-quarter-inch waistband was fastened by two sets of hooks and eyes, one above the other, two and a half inches in from the end of the band and then, one hook and bar at the edge. That way, the skirt lay evenly on the waist, and the zipper closure was secure. As the styles changed and I became more mature, the skirt length grew a bit longer than my mother's 1970s and 1980s

styles, extending to mid knee. Sometimes now, when I am seeking a match
for a blazer jacket or sweater, I don one
of her little black skirts, which still fit
me, and I relish the sensation of slip-
ping my hands into the hidden pocket
wells on the side seams, a trademark of
all her skirt designs.

A little black skirt and jacket

She made the much-anticipated move
to Genesis House, the subsidized elderly housing complex, in the summer of
1998. By then, she was eighty-five years
old and had lost much of the strength
required of a good sewer who must con-
stantly set herself on the floor for fittings. She must then rise from
the floor using her legs and torso and use her strong arms and
hands for cutting, ironing, pinning, and maneuvering the sewing
needle. Still, she maintained a few faithful customers and continued to sew for them and me and for my daughter.

Exhibiting only a few
sparks of genius over the
next few years in origi-
nal creations, she devoted
much of her sewing time to
alterations. No longer able
to accommodate a separate
sewing room in her small,
one-bedroom apartment,
she placed her sewing ma-
chine against a wall in her

Sidonia and the author on the latter's fifti-
eth birthday wearing clothes "by Sidonia":
a cotton jersey flowered over-blouse and
matelassé white cotton suit with appliquéd
embroidered flowers

new living room. Her reputation as a talented seamstress had followed her, and sometimes the staff and residents of Genesis House asked her to perform simple alterations.

Still, she missed the bustle of regular customers entering and exiting her apartment and the challenge of their innumerable sewing projects. She was not only alone then, but also lonely, an emotion she had not allowed herself earlier in her life. Although surrounded by other residents in the complex, she made few friends. Aside from the occasional bingo game, she left her apartment only to go to a luncheon at the nearby Jewish Community Center, go on her weekly food shopping excursions, and, once in a while, give a presentation about her Holocaust experiences at the nearby Hatikvah Holocaust Education Center, named for the Club Hatikvah of my youth.

As she approached ninety, she decided to return to the synagogue. Never known for her attendance at either Shabbat or holiday services, she became obsessed with participation in the festive celebrations advertised in the synagogue newsletter. I noticed that sometimes she would even forego her visit to us to attend a Hanukkah or Purim party or the joyful celebration of Simchat Torah, when the annual cycle of Torah reading ends and begins anew. It had been many years — in fact, not since I was a child — since she had taken part in these Jewish holidays. I found it distinctly strange that, suddenly, she felt an urgency to return to the rituals and traditional observances of her faith. I suspect she retained her ambivalence about God and her anger at the abandonment of his faithful servants, yet perhaps her renewed observance allowed her to reach back to her youthful days when her family had rejoiced together in their Jewishness. For the most part, however, when I went to visit her, she seemed so withdrawn and isolated that I felt guilty about not taking her home to live with me.

Han, sometime a few days go by and I don't see anybody. I try to find vays to kill a day, to make it go by faster, but it's so hard, she would say with anguish written on her face, starting to use the expression "kill a day" as though to her a day had to be attacked and slain to put behind her.

Ma, would you like to come to Connecticut to live with me? I asked, already knowing her answer.

No, Hani, you know I have to stay in Springfield. Dis is da place I live for so long. You and da kits, you are mine life, but I'm used to Springfield.

One time, when I drove away from her apartment, I thought back to a statement she had made in the psychiatrist's office a few years earlier, just after she mourned the loss of her sister, who would have been "somebody" in her life. She followed that comment with this:

If not for Hani, I vouldn't be alive.

Then Dr. Laub asked, *Do you mean that otherwise you might have committed suicide?*

No, I mean she da von who help me in dis country. She da von who help me be a mentsh, to make a life here. If I didn't have her, I couldn't survive.

I knew when she expressed those words, hearing them for the first time, that I had given meaning to her life after the heartbreak of the Holocaust and its aftermath. Despite our mutual efforts to protect each other from pain by withholding our true feelings, or maybe because of it, we had formed a perfect unit, just the two of us. Each time I left her tiny apartment, I knew I was her lifeline to the universe.

With my altered feelings about my mother in mind, I found the document in my store of stolen letters that clarified the circumstances of my birth more than any other. Folded over several times, without an envelope, the document was a three-page letter written on lightweight paper in either very dark blue or black ink. Translated from the Hungarian in 1999, the letter reads as follows:

December 27, 1948

Dear Szidi—

We received your letter, which I will try to answer in a straightforward, objective way. I must remark that people experience many things in their lives, but I never heard of anything quite like your case until now.

I see from your letter that you admit that you are responsible. I cannot even imagine what you might have been thinking at the first moment when you began a relationship with such a young boy. I have a clear idea from your letter, and I must express my opinion.

Shmule left three years ago, and at that time he could not and did not know about women. He was very inexperienced. As a man myself, I understand a young boy finding a woman and not thinking about the consequences, but only about living for the moment. The question is, where have you been, because three years ago, you were already old enough to think rationally and knew what it meant to live with a man, the possibility of having a child, and if it happened, as it usually does, why did you not get an abortion in time? I cannot imagine what you thought, because, you know, you cannot be the wife of such a young boy.

I have heard of cases where the woman is older than the man by a few years. The man might be 25 or 30 and the woman is older. But I have never heard of a case of a boy who is 18 or 19 and the woman is 27 or 28, so it is a very big thing. For this misfortune, you must bear all the consequences, and you have to solve the question regarding the way to find a husband who suits you and find happiness in your life. You should not try to convince Shmule to marry you because he is already so unfortunate to have something like this [happen] in his young years. Even though he has made a mistake too, the responsibility is only yours. You cannot wish him to be unfortunate his whole life.

How can you think that a child should have the responsibility of raising a child? It was very curious for us why the boys did not want to come here. We were thinking of many reasons, but never about such disaster. Unfortunately, the child exists, but she is yours. No boy thinks of a child at his age.

You should find a husband who suits you. Men will marry women with a child, and in that case, you can be happier. We have heard of husbands and wives divorcing even after having several children together, and in this case, you are not even married. You do not have to make such a big tragedy of it, but start solving the problem.

I hope you understand our point of view, and we wish you good luck and happiness.

Gershon

So there it was, the guilt and shame my mother had carried inside her for so many years, explained in three pages of a fifty-year-old letter from someone who appeared to be my father's "objective" relative. The "tall, skinny kid" apparently was just that, a teenager with whom my mother had entered into a relationship that was doomed from the start. When I was conceived in 1946, my mother, who continued to lie about her age, was really thirty-three years old, and my father was no more than nineteen. In those times, that age difference between a man and woman was considered indecent.

My mother seemed to accept the burden of blame underscored by the writer of this letter, "For this misfortune, you must bear all the consequences. . . . Even though he has made a mistake too, the responsibility is only yours." My mother did acknowledge her responsibility, affirmed in my video of her in 1998, just a year before I read this letter. That burden stayed with her until the day she died.

I sometimes look at the letter. I cannot help but regret all those years I spent hating my mother for her unyielding pride and her inability to share with me the true story of my birth. Its words not only explained why my father had never attempted to know me, but also the courage my mother possessed in having the child she had conceived in a displaced persons camp and in raising her truly alone, with no assistance from anyone. The real meaning of "I don't care," her often-repeated expression in the previous year's video, suddenly fell into place. After losing everyone she had ever loved, she made the choice to keep the baby who would extend her family into the future. Having made her decision, there was no turning back. She did not care anymore about those who had stood in her way.

I ceased any further attempts to contact my father. In any case, I learned that he passed away a few years later, sometime in the year preceding the summer of 2005. My son, Stephen, had attempted to contact his elusive, long-lost grandfather on a trip to Israel. In the process, he discovered his grandfather had died. Upon learning the news, I felt only sympathy for the man who had missed knowing his first daughter. After reading the illuminating letter, I had already discovered that I no longer needed him to feel complete. Indeed, I realized I was as complete as any human being could desire.

My mother, often without my knowing it, had crafted a daughter who managed to turn heads with her breathtaking clothes, attained a high level of education just as my mother had desired, earned the respect of colleagues in her profession, and bore two children to extend the Perlstein lineage. It was in the instant I finished reading the letter that I belatedly began to love my mother in the unconditional and spiritual way that I never could express before, the same way she had always loved me. That is how I loved her for the rest of her life.

25 Hems

The hem is the last detail, the step that completes a garment. — "Hems," page 98

The clock on my microwave oven showed that it was already 10:30 a.m. My mother, the most punctual person I have ever met, was a half hour late for her Sunday visit. I phoned her several times, but there was no answer. Perplexed at what could have detained her, I imagined all sorts of horrific circumstances that might have occurred during her ride from Springfield to Vernon.

Just then, the phone rang. I picked it up, and an unfamiliar man's voice asked whether my name was Hanna Marcus.

Yes, that's me, I responded.

We have your mother at our doughnut shop over here in Hazardville. She seems to be lost. She showed us a slip of paper with your name and phone number. Could you come and get her?

Okay, thanks. I should be there in less than a half hour, I responded, surprised that my mother had ended up at a doughnut shop in Hazardville, Connecticut, not the usual route she took to my house.

When I arrived, she was waiting on a stool, shaking her head, muttering that she had somehow taken a wrong turn, found herself in a strange town, and had no choice but to stop to ask for help. Troubled by my mother's inability to remember the route to my home, I gently asked her whether she would be able to follow me back to my house in her car. She nodded yes, and I slowly led her on the back-road journey to Vernon, peering out of my rear view mirror every few seconds.

As I look back, this event probably signaled the mental decline that followed. In the beginning, she denied her diminished mental capacity. *Han, it vas just a mistake. Don't vorry, I just took a wrong turn*, she told me, hoping I would buy this rationale.

But ma, you've driven to my house so many times over the years, and you always followed the same route. I can't help but be concerned, I said, but I was reluctant to take steps to snatch her independence from her. I allowed her to continue driving, letting her impose her will yet again, but in my heart, I knew I should not have permitted it.

It was only a few months later that she drove her car, whose registration and insurance listed me as the owner, too close to the right-hand curb and smashed into a parked car on Dickenson Street, just about a mile from her apartment at Genesis House. She was in shock when she called me after arriving back at her apartment to tell me what happened, identifying the location of the accident as near the "corner of Brookline Avenue and Chestnut Street," on the other side of the city, where we had lived when we first came to America. She had not stopped at the scene but continued driving, afraid to confront the owners of the parked automobile.

Together in my car, we traced back the route my mother had driven before the accident and, sure enough, we found a parked vehicle on the corner of Dickenson Street and Texel Drive — not Brookline and Chestnut — that looked as though it had been bashed in the rear, glass from the rear lights still scattered along the road. As I stopped near the scene of the accident, the owner came out of his home. He had witnessed my mother careening into his car, shouted and waved at her to stop, but she did not look in his direction, continuing to drive straight ahead.

A few days later, after working out the details of the damages with the other party, I advised my mother of the insurance adjuster's verdict: her car was destroyed and unfixable. My verdict: we would not purchase another vehicle to replace it.

Han, don't do dis to me, please. Vhat can I do mitout a car? Let's fix da car. I'm sure dey can do it, she pleaded.

The car was fifteen years old, ma. It's just not possible. I know it's hard, but I think it would be a good idea to stop driving and take senior transportation to the places you want to go, I said, sounding tentative. I was not used to being in a power position with my mother.

Please, Hani, please, she continued for the next few weeks. *I'm okay to drive. It vas just von accident. Everybody has von accident.*

She was right. Everybody has one accident, and she had a close-to-impeccable driving record since obtaining her license at age forty-eight. During those forty years, she drove the breadth of the city, from Baystate Medical Center, where the old Springfield Hospital stood, all the way to the Longmeadow line, and from Memorial Square to the Eastfield Mall, rarely requiring directions. *I just go vhere da car take me, Hani,* she said proudly. She had owned and driven only three cars: the 1961 beige Chevy Impala, the 1974 lime green Oldsmobile Cutlass, and finally, the 1987 navy blue Buick Century she had demolished finally in *the* accident. She had made each vehicle last for more than a dozen years, maintaining them in remarkable condition. Next to her sewing machines, her automobiles were her most prized possessions.

I wanted to accede to my mother's wishes. I knew her agonizing loneliness would only accelerate if she could not have a car. However, thinking of her safety and that of others, I was adamant about not replacing her car. Not surprisingly, she did not go down without a fight, insisting she be allowed to prove her driving proficiency. Brenda and I accompanied her as her driving skill was tested at the Weldon Rehabilitation Hospital, which is part of Mercy Medical Center.

After failing the evaluation owing to slow upper- and lower-body reaction times, she spewed venom at the occupational therapist who administered the test in the simulated automobile laboratory. For the first time, at age eighty-nine, she used her survival of the Holocaust as a defense for what she viewed as an unjust appraisal.

You know, almost sixty years ago, I vas in a concentration camp, she shouted, *an I survived. If I live trough dat, I tink you should let me drive. Dis test don't prove I can't drive. I know I can.*

I have to go by the test results. I'm so sorry, the therapist replied, shaken by my mother's words. My mother wanted to say more, but Brenda and I apologized to the therapist and hustled her out of the room, disconcerted by her sudden outburst.

The abrupt loss of her independence, represented by her driver's license, seemed to dislodge the tight clamp she had held on her anger — at the Nazis, at God, and now at me. *It vasn't dat bad,* she insisted, accusing me of lying to her about the severity of the car's damage. *I can drive it just da vay it is.*

It was an uncomfortable time for both of us. She understood that I had the power to influence her independence, which she had always cherished above everything. Yet she loved me too much to allow her anger at me to rule the day, and finally, she gave in to the inevitable. My guilt initially at playing a part in limiting her autonomy gave way to the consolation of knowing that, in the face of her rapid physical deterioration and dementia, I had made the correct decision. It did not, however, save me from the agony of watching this once strong, clever, and prideful woman lose her grip on life.

She started using the senior van, but she just could never get used to waiting until a scheduled time for the driver to arrive. On several occasions, I heard tales about her walking to the Jewish Community Center in bitter snow and ice when the driver was only five minutes late. Visions of a ninety-year-old woman trekking through the snow just to eat lunch and interact with other human beings kept me up at night. Within a year of the car accident, in June of 2003, she was admitted to the Jewish Nursing Home of Western Massachusetts.

As though everyone there knew that sewing was her life's blood, and that thread, needle, fabric, and measuring tools were her veins and arteries, the nursing home arranged for her sewing machine to be placed in its activity room. Beside it, on the floor, lay her wicker basket with her favorite sewing items.

I distributed most of her belongings, other than some framed pictures and articles of clothing, donating the fabric remnants and the few furnishings from her apartment to various charities. Many were from her first days in Springfield, such as the blonde bedroom set we once shared. I took the silver-plated candelabra home with me, along with some pots and pans, her Rosenthal china, another small china set purchased at the old Forbes and Wallace department store, and some of her remaining pictures and letters. It struck me that she had not acquired very many possessions in the fifty years she had lived in the United States.

It is painful for me to think back on those last three years of my mother's life as she struggled to retain her dignity and self-respect. She liked to think that she was not really in a nursing home but at the Jewish Community Center, having her meals and participating in activities, and then driving home to her own apartment. She would be disappointed when I left for home after visiting her. *Han, I have to go too. It's getting dark, and I have to drive home,* she would say.

No, ma, you have a room here. You don't have to drive home. You have your own bed right here.

She sobbed and begged me not to leave her, like a kindergartner grabbing her mother's arm, coaxing her to stay with her at school.

Assigned to a semiprivate room, my mother had difficulty sharing the small space with someone else and was vocal about her displeasure to all who could hear. True to her stubborn character, she irrationally insisted that her roommate move out, since she had been there first. *Han, dis vas my room before she came. Vhy can't she move? Maybe dere is anoder room for her*, she asked me with total sincerity.

Your roommate is too sick to move, ma. The nurses have offered you a chance to move into your own private room, but you have to make the decision right away, I advised her. But she would not budge.

We were at a stalemate for a while, until I arrived one day and, with the cooperation of the staff, packed up her things and moved her to a private room two doors down, near the nurses' station. My mother just looked at me as I completed this task, not sure why I was so insistent, still waiting for her severely ill roommate to make the first move. But the willfulness about her that I had grown to love sometimes still got in the way of her happiness. By then, however, I had developed the stomach to take matters into my own hands.

I noticed that she had been assigned to a small table in the cafeteria, where she sat by herself most of the time unless I was there during meals to sit with her. Nearby, other women and a few men sat at round tables for four to six residents, some of whom I recognized as members of *di grine* of my youth, now wizened by age.

I could often hear a pin drop during mealtimes, the silence sometimes broken by music from a boom box or a conversation among the nurse's aides. I never asked why my mother was sitting alone, perhaps sensing that she was more content that way, never having learned to socialize with ease. She had been lonely before moving to the nursing home, but after so many years of living alone, she seemed to find living with constant human interaction difficult.

She stopped calling me about a year after her arrival, no longer able to recall my phone number or to find the piece of paper on which it was written. I discontinued calling her as well since she was never in her room. The nurses' aides had moved her to the hallway or to the crowd of residents who sat in their wheelchairs or in chairs near their walkers in the television room, watching an aging Andy Griffith still solving murders on *Matlock*. She had a walker for the first two years of her three-year stay, but after repeated falls and a fractured pelvic bone, she was confined to a wheelchair.

She retained her eye for fashion and grooming during her last years, often leaning over from her wheelchair to grab the errant sleeve or hem of a nurse's aide, tucking the frayed edge back inside. It happened so often that the staff could tell when she was looking at their clothing and automatically just walked over to her to receive her "alterations." She also maintained a kind of celebrity status when visitors or residents recognized her in the hallways or television room. *That's Mrs. Perlstein, the seamstress, who made my daughter's bat mitzvah dress. Hi, Mrs. Perlstein, remember me?* Even when she did not remember, she smiled back and nodded and held her head up high.

Whenever I came to visit — which eventually was almost every day of the week — she was stunned to see me. When I arrived, she always put her hands to her face, covered her eyes, and slowly took her hands down, saying something like this: *Hani, vhy you here? It's snowing out. You shouldn't drive on a day like dis.* I knew it was her way of showing her excitement at seeing me. I would respond: *It's barely snowing, ma, I wanted to see you. I miss you.*

How da kits? she questioned. Then she asked about my Catholic partner, for whom she had developed affection, satisfied that he was taking good care of her daughter. I did not have the heart to tell her we had gone our separate ways.

> *Everyone's fine, ma. How are you today?*
> *I'm okay, but I'm vondering, Han, vhat are da interest rates now?*
> *Well, they are very low today, about 2 percent,* I replied.
> *Two percent? Dat's just terrible. I don't believe it.*
> *It's true, ma. But at least the money is safe in the bank.*

For the first two years at the nursing home, she wanted to continue to "visit" her money at the bank, as she always had in the past. Once a month, I signed her out of the home and drove her to a nearby bank, where she had a safe deposit box and where her Social Security checks went by direct deposit. Although most of her Social Security money each month was owed to the nursing home in partial payment for its care, she did not know that, and I did not tell her. I sent a check from my own checking account each month equivalent to the amount owed and let her cash her Social Security to keep in her safe deposit box. She had to believe that she still had money, to see it and touch it, and I would do anything to protect her from all undue anxiety or disappointment.

The safe deposit box held the same items each time we looked: a few envelopes with some twenty dollar bills inside; a couple of small metal boxes that formerly housed throat lozenges, now filled with JFK silver half dollars and Eisenhower silver dollars; two-dollar bills; and her citizenship papers.

Tucked in a corner of the box, underneath all the other contents, was a small manila envelope containing seventeen vivid black-and-white two- by three-inch photos of the members of the *Sonderkommando*, the team of concentration camp prisoners that was assigned to dispose of corpses. They were standing in various positions beside a crematorium, handling dead bodies with a tool that resembled large forceps, grabbing the cadavers around their necks and feet, lifting them to the oven opening. Other snapshots depicted cadavers piled high, one on top of the other, some of the bodies naked and some still dressed in their striped prisoner's clothing. One picture haunts me even more than the others. The dead faces are shown up close, among them the angelic face of a child.

Having seen these pictures many times during my life, I no longer needed to ask what they were or how she obtained them. I knew she kept them in her safe deposit box all those years because they were in a category all by themselves, too horrible to keep in her nightstand drawer with the rest of her photos. She was well aware of their impact and sometimes said, *If ve ever be so poor dat ve have no money, maybe somebody vould pay us for dese pictures,* but I knew she had no intention of ever selling them.

She often repeated the story of a physician survivor she had met during her time at the Bergen Belsen displaced persons camp who had befriended a Hungarian soldier stationed at Auschwitz. The soldier took photographs during his assignment there and hid his camera underground at the camp. After the war, he returned to find his camera and developed the film. The physician obtained twenty copies of the photos, distributing them to twenty of his friends, my mother apparently among them.

To tell the truth, I tried not to look at these pictures too closely when I was younger because the images were simply too terrifying. The workers in the Kommando appeared stiff and morose, looking down toward the emaciated cadavers as though posing for the poster of a chilling horror movie. The photos of the mounds of corpses lying on the ground or piled onto trucks were beyond my comprehension. Not until I inherited those pictures and spent time viewing them, not inside a safe deposit cubicle but rather in my own home, could I fathom their true meaning.

As I looked closely at the seventeen pictures, I realized, finally, why I had never been able to wholly embrace my mother's stories. It was not only her detached, dispassionate method of delivering her accounts that made them seem unreachable and intangible to me. It was the sheer magnitude of the violence and brutality they evidenced that I long tried to shut out. Avoiding those images for so long prevented me from acknowledging the callous truth of what had happened to my mother and her family. I realized then that all of it was true, all the details of the "evaporation" of the sisters and brothers, mothers and fathers and children, and uncles and aunts. They were lost to the last great Jewish community of Europe that was Hungary, the last country whose Jews were torn from their roots and delivered to their deaths during World War II.

At the nursing home, my mother had taken to hoarding food from her meals and saving it to give to me when I visited. After eating just a little bit, she stacked most of her meals in mounds of food groups I called the roast beef parfait: mashed potatoes at the bottom, topped by roast beef, topped with vegetables, topped with canned peaches, topped with cake, topped with salt and sugar packets, all jammed into a few milk cartons or plastic beverage cups with caps. Initially she put the food into a small dormitory refrigerator in her room, and with a bit of intrigue that my mother thoroughly enjoyed, I would remove the food in plastic bags at every visit.

Vatch out, Hani, da nurse is looking on us, she advised me as we approached her refrigerator for this important caper. *I gonna stand here so she can't see us fun da door.*

Fine, ma, I responded, holding my plastic bag and hastily emptying the contents of the refrigerator into it, sometimes using three or four bags.

Hani, be careful mit da food. Don't trow it like dat into da bag. Vhat's wrong mit you? she asked, in a highly irritated tone.

Sorry, ma, just trying to do it as fast as possible.

Then, I walked down the corridor, trying to hide the bags amid my coat and purse, hoping no one would notice them, ballooned out with food scraps — as though someone might really care.

She was satisfied that I was taking home these leftovers to enjoy at a later date, supposedly saving me from cooking. When Brenda and her family came to visit her on their weekly visits to the nursing home, she was proud to offer them their share of food scraps as well. Of course, we all threw our care packages away soon after retrieving them, but that was one of our secrets from her. Later, when her dementia progressed further, the hoarded food was packed directly into her pocketbook, where it saturated the inner lining and soaked anything else that was inside. It all reminded me of how she had stolen the turnip from underground while in a concentration camp and relished it with her bunkmates.

In the end, it was a hem that told me my mother would not live much longer. Brenda and I consistently brought clothing for alterations even if they did not require any, but pretending that they did, trying to keep her alive as long as possible because, for her, to stop sewing was to stop breathing. She was too weak to perform the fittings she had insisted upon in the past. She took our word about the amount of shortening or lengthening the garment required. *Just let the hem down all the way, ma,* I would say, eliminating the need for her to measure it on my body. But I noticed that she had delayed hemming a pair of pants for many weeks, and I wondered why she had postponed doing the work.

Are these the pants I brought you a few weeks ago to be lengthened? I asked her, observing them in her closet, mixed in with the few items that were hers and some that belonged to other residents, whose clothes would often mistakenly land in her closet after a trip to the laundry.

Yeh, Han, I gonna do it for you. Next veek I gonna have dem ready, she replied, pretending it was no problem.

Okay ma, but if you don't want to do the hem, that's all right, I said, trying to alleviate any pressure.

No, don't vorry. I gonna have it for you.

Finally, after another two weeks passed, she presented me with the pants. When I looked inside to check the hem, the gray pants had been stitched with yellow thread in a pattern of large "X's." Compared with her inconspicuous and precise hemstitches of the past, this one looked nothing less than grotesque. I knew immediately that it was the last piece of sewing she would ever complete.

Thanks, ma. I'm glad you finished the hem, I commented without hesitation.

Dat's okay, Hani, she responded, looking down at the floor, perhaps realizing that she had revealed more than she would have liked.

During the last few months of her life, she lost so much weight that she no longer resembled the big-boned, sturdy woman I remembered. Since she weighed less than 90 pounds, the dentures she had worn since shortly after arriving in the United States no longer fit her shrunken face. She wore them less and less, which warbled her speech, collapsed her already hollow cheeks, and diminished her ability to chew food.

Everybody here, dey can't vait for lunch, to see vhat it look like, she said to me one time during her last two weeks, *but, you know, Han, I don't care anymore.*

To make matters worse, her food arrived pureed during that time, the staff concerned that she would not otherwise be able to swallow her meals. I picked up the unappetizing, totally unrecognizable, pulverized chicken on a spoon and attempted to place it in her mouth.

No, Hanele, no, she said softly, calling me by the name she had not used in forty years, *I don't vant it.*

Her dementia had accelerated so rapidly that, at times, she was unable to speak coherently or rationally. Nonetheless, she never forgot my face or the faces of her grandchildren, Brenda's husband, Michael, or her great-grandchild, Lauren. In her last few days, her instinctive will to live was so strong that she made attempts at raising her fragile body out of bed, facing in my direction as though she could sense my presence.

When the nursing home's rabbi entered the room on Friday afternoon, my mother was visibly startled and seemed to listen intently as the rabbi asked whether she would like to sing her favorite Shabbos song. I wondered what melody constituted my mother's favorite Shabbos song, not remembering whether she had ever shared that preference with me. When the rabbi began to sing in her comforting, assured manner, I recognized it immediately. My mother's face stood riveted on the rabbi's mouth as she sang:

Shalom Aleichem, Malachei ha-Sharet, Malachei Elyon (Peace be unto you, O Ministering Angels, Messengers of the Most High).

I recognized it as one of the songs she had sung with her fellow prisoners in Auschwitz as they hunkered down to clean the latrines. It seemed fitting that the last song she would ever hear was the one that had given her solace during the most demoralizing period of her life. I cried for the first time during those last days as I sang this song with the rabbi, hovering over my mother's body and holding her hand.

Although her eyes were open, they looked like cardboard cutouts pasted onto the eye socket, blocking out any glimmer of inner light. She grabbed my arm in a tight squeeze, as though to say,

Hanele, I'm asking you to help me get out of here. Vhat's wrong mit you? Do you hear me?

I heard her as clear as anyone could and admired her more in those last five days than I ever had in my life. She had not lost her character at the end. She was still the determined, obstinate woman whom I had only reluctantly loved in my early years and later grew to understand, revere, and love with all my heart. She died on Mother's Day, 2006, at age ninety-three, waiting for me to arrive back at her bedside after a few restless hours of sleep, to lift her tongue to the roof of her mouth and stop breathing.

26 Thread

Threads, like fabrics, are often treated with finishes to impart special qualities and improve performance. — "Thread and Needles," page 164

The nursing home staff called the next week to inform me that they had moved my mother's things out of her room in order to prepare it for a new resident. I had barely finished sitting *shiva* when someone else was already moving into her room. Initially shaken by the realization that other lives dared to continue in the face of my enormous loss, I tried to make the necessary practical decisions, postponing the emotional pain for as long as possible.

What would you like to do with your mother's clothes? the social worker asked.

Just donate or discard them, I advised. Most of her clothes were worn out or soiled, and I had already taken the items I wanted to keep before she even entered the nursing facility.

Please store the other things, and my son-in-law and I will be there soon to retrieve them.

When I arrived a few days later, the receptionist directed me to the storage area, located behind the main building. I braced myself as I went in to inspect what remained of my mother's three-year stay at the nursing home. An older African-American woman, whom I recognized from some of my visits, greeted me with a comforting smile and told me that my mother had been a special lady. She led me to a room of boxes teeming with clothing, knickknacks, and countless remote controls, the remnants of living souls who had lost their lives to chronic illness and old age.

She pointed out the few possessions that belonged to my mother: an antique wooden Pfaff console sewing machine, still threaded; a brown wicker sewing basket filled with thread, needles, patterns, trim, and seam bindings; and a small portable television set. As I waited in the dark hallway near the doors leading out to the loading dock for my son-in-law, Mike, to arrive with his van, I took stock of what my mother had left after ninety-three years as her estate. Combined with the items I had taken when she left her apartment at Genesis House, it amounted to a few household items and two German-designed sewing machines. Always, above everything else, there were her precious, life-sustaining sewing machines.

I often hear my mother's voice now, reprimanding me for allowing her sewing machines, the Köhler and the Pfaff, to sit back to back in my basement, lying dormant and forlorn, waiting for someone to bring them back to life. I have never touched the scissors, spools of thread, measuring tools, extra bobbins, or other sewing notions stored in their drawers. With my lack of interest and talent, there's no chance that I will ever master the sewing technique required to put them to good use, yet I cannot bear to release them to someone else. Perhaps my granddaughters, Lauren and Sydney, my aunt's and mother's namesakes, will take up sewing as they grow older, and the machines will whir once again.

Although she never wanted me to live alone, always reassured by the thought that someone was taking care of me, I am nevertheless often alone these days. Yet, I am comforted by my recollections of the Hungarian Perlstein clan, whose memory may also have steadied my mother during all the years she sat by herself in her sewing room pushing thread through a needle.

In many ways, the threads she wove gave me the family I did not have as a child. Her stories created a tapestry rich with colors and textures so vibrant, they live for me in a place that transcends imagination. I can see their faces and feel their character as though they were alive: Szeren surrounded by her books; Dezso embroiled in a top-secret adventure; Etel patiently listening to the stories of others; the beautiful Laura at her sewing machine; Simon negotiating the best price for his goods; Hani tending her garden; and finally, Sidonia, perched on the floor looking up at me as she pinned a hem. I feel that I am one of them.

Since my mother's death, I occasionally think about what would have happened to her if she had not given birth to a child under those impossible circumstances in a displaced persons camp. Would she have had a more normal life, perhaps a spouse, and a couple of kids, and would she have become the kind of married baleboste of which she often spoke? As I sit at my desk and write, sometimes I hear the words, *I'm sorry,* coming without warning from somewhere inside me. *I'm sorry, ma, that I got in the way of your happiness,* I say to her.

But would she have been happier? Maybe, but she would not have had the particular seamstress-model partnership that we created, nor exhibited the great talent she portrayed to her local universe through me. Perhaps no one would have listened as passionately and without interruption to the stories of her childhood or to her horrible tales of the Holocaust. Perhaps no one would have been willing to accede to her wishes time after time, to meet her high expectations, or to be the embodiment of her creative dreams. I like to think that I was, indeed, the one who helped her to be a *mentsh,* as she had once said in the psychiatrist's office. And she, no doubt, did the same for me.

Sometimes I venture downstairs to the closet in the basement filled to the brim with the clothes my mother fashioned over the last two decades of her life. I examine the stitched threads as I never viewed them when they were first constructed, and I am overwhelmed with love for her. I am as much her product as those garments, stitched surely with a steady hand, a continuation of the thread that seamed early twentieth century Hungary to twenty-first-century America. It is the gift that made her such a worthy representative of the millions of seamstresses who lost their lives to unabashed evil and indifference.

Late one night, alone and unable to sleep, picturing my mother's sober, resolute face before me as we sat at her kitchen table, I took one of my frequent walks downstairs and stood at the entrance of the basement closet. As I looked at and touched the garments again and recollected the fabric selection and fitting of each one, I finally came to terms with why my mother was never able to share the whole truth about my identity.

It had to be more than just her shame at having committed a mistake, a lapse in judgment at the worst moment of her life. I am convinced that it had everything to do with her lessons on standing up straight. *Stand up straight, Hanele. Put your shoulders back or else I gonna have a crooked hem.* It was the most common refrain she ever uttered to me. To her, it meant more than just fitting an article of clothing so that it lay perfectly on my body. It meant infusing and then reinforcing my self-esteem and strength of character. She was determined not to let the circumstances of my birth limit my development into a confident, accomplished, and content member of society. I understand her motives so much better now. I hope she can hear me when I say, *See ma, I am standing up straight now. You were right.*

Epilogue

I traveled to the Kesser Israel Cemetery on Wilbraham Road in Springfield two years after my mother's death. Although I had diligently recited the Kaddish prayers in her memory every day in the year after she died, knowing she would have been pleased with my newly found devotion to ritual, I had not visited her grave often. Perhaps it was too difficult to face the certainty of my loss. It was on the Sunday between Rosh Hashanah, the Jewish New Year, and Yom Kippur, the Day of Atonement, a traditional time for graveside visits. As I stood outside the gates, my eyes gazed at the sea of grave markers and settled on the rose-colored granite stone that bears my mother's Hebrew name, *Shasha Bat Shimon v'Chana* (Shasha, daughter of Simon and Chana) and identifies her: *A Woman with Golden Hands*.

Then, I encountered the elderly cemetery keeper. *Can I help you find the grave you are seeking? If you tell me the name, maybe I can help*, he asked.

I know where the grave is, thanks, I responded. *Her name was Sidonia Perlstein*.

Oh, of course, my wife and I knew you both when you first came to Springfield. My wife was a social worker with Jewish Social Services.

Wow! That's really something. It was such a long time ago, I said. *Thanks for telling me*.

He turned to walk away, but then, turning around again with a questioning look, he asked, *The seamstress, right?* As I nodded, my mouth curled up into a slight smile, marveling at the reach of Sidonia's thread.

First row left to right, the author, Sydney, Lauren, and Stephen's wife, Elena, Second row: Brenda's husband, Michael, Stephen, and Brenda, 2010

Addendum

I often wondered during my childhood about what really happened to my mother and her family during the Holocaust. Did my Uncle Dezso lose his life in Auschwitz, as we had always thought? Was he as tall as my mother remembered? What was my Aunt Laura's exact fate? What was her physical description? What really happened to Simon, Szeren, and Etel, my grandfather and aunts? What about my great Uncle Shayme, who brought the Passover food to the ghetto so that the inhabitants could celebrate their special holiday? And since we could not find Kis Etu in her hometown in Hungary, where did she go and was she still alive? These were questions I never dreamed would be answered.

Yet, as I finished writing the core story of *Sidonia's Thread* in 2009, I learned that perhaps it was all possible. I could find some of the information that, in some cases, my mother would never have wanted to know, and some she would have rejoiced in discovering.

The fifty million pages of records amassed by the Allies after World War II about more than seventeen million victims of the Holocaust were finally released and made accessible to the public starting in 2008. Stored for more than sixty years in archives located in the small town of Bad Arolson, Germany, the records contain the Nazi's meticulously detailed information: transportation lists, labor records, camp registration books, and death records, as well as postwar lists of survivors in displaced persons camps. Administered by the International Tracing Service, a branch of the International

270 Hanna Perlstein Marcus

Committee of the Red Cross, the records were released according to an agreement by the eleven nations that had overseen its operation since the end of World War II. The United States Holocaust Memorial Museum assumed the role of processing information requests from American survivors and their families and acted as a liaison with the International Tracing Service (ITS).

Excited by the news, I applied for information about many of the characters mentioned in this memoir. Starting with the immediate members of the Perlstein family, including my mother, her sisters Laura, Etel, and Szeren, her brother Dezso, and father Simon, I tried to remember as many details as I could of their first names, various surnames, nicknames, places of residence, and concentration camps in which they were confined. I decided to add my great Uncle Shayme and Kis Etu to the list as well.

The results of my requests, which began to emerge in mid-2009, were sometimes predictable and yet sometimes considerably surprising, not only because of the new pieces of information they generated, but also because of the sheer enormity and detail of the records. This addendum is my way of sharing the revelations that have added so much to the thread and texture of a family my mother tried to keep alive for me in her stories. The findings were as follows:

My grandfather, Simon Perlstein, a resident of Dámóc, Hungary, was interned at the ghetto at Sátoraljaújhely. He was deported to the Auschwitz concentration camp in May 1944. The ITS search for him yielded no results, consistent with a deportee who had been exterminated soon after his arrival. No prisoner number had therefore been assigned.

My aunt, Szeren Perlstein Frankfurt, a resident of Dámóc, Hungary, was interned at the ghetto at Sátoraljaújhely. She was deported to the Auschwitz concentration camp in May 1944. The ITS search for her yielded no results.

My aunt, Etel Perlstein Deutsch, a resident of Dámóc and Sátoraljaújhely, Hungary, was interned at the ghetto at Sátoraljaújhely. She was deported to the Auschwitz concentration camp in May 1944. The ITS search for her yielded no results.

My great uncle, Shayme Perlstein, also known as Samuel, Sajma, and Shemaya, a resident of Dámóc, Hungary, was interned at the ghetto at Sátoraljaújhely. He was deported to the Auschwitz concentration camp in May 1944. The ITS search for him yielded no results.

My aunt, Laura Perlstein, a resident of Dámóc, Hungary, was interned at the ghetto at Sátoraljaújhely. She was deported to the Auschwitz concentration camp on May 20, 1944. She remained at Auschwitz until July 27, 1944, when she was among eight hundred Hungarian-Jewish women who were transferred from Auschwitz-Birkenau to the Dachau concentration camp, where she arrived on August 1, 1944. A standard questionnaire administered to her by Dachau camp officials, completed in ink, shows biographical and descriptive information. As translated, it reads in part:

> Dachau concentration camp [*Konzentrationslager Dachau*] …
>   Prisoner Number 86795
> *Perlstein Laura, born on January 6, 1914, in Dámóc*
> *Occupation: dressmaker* [sneiderin (sic) for 'schneiderin']
> *Country of origin: Hungary. Status: Unmarried*
> *Parents' names: Simon and Klein Hani. Place of residence:*
>   *Dámóc*
> *Height: 160* [centimeters, or 5′3″], *Shape: normal, Face:*
>   *round, Eyes: blue, Nose: normal, Mouth: normal, Ears:*
>   *normal, Teeth: defective, Hair: brown, Language: Hungarian*
> *Arrested on: May 20, 1944, in Sátoraljaújhely*
> *Arrived on August 1, 1944. Sent from Department: Auschwitz*
>   *concentration camp*

Laura Perlstein's Dachau questionnaire. Courtesy of the United States Holocaust Memorial Museum and the International Tracing Service

The lovely Laura had blue eyes and brown hair with a round face, though at the point of entry at Dachau, apparently her teeth were "defective." Her questionnaire accurately describes her as a seamstress, just as my mother was, one of the most common occupations for Jewish women in Europe. Yet, it also inaccurately offers her birth year as 1914, the false age she and my mother began to circulate as they moved through various concentration camps. The last documented entry for Laura Perlstein shows that on December 17, 1944, she was on a list of fourteen hundred people sent from Dachau to the Bergen Belsen concentration camp. Her trail ends there; no date of death is cited.

My mother, Sidonia Perlstein, resident of Dámóc, Hungary, interned at the ghetto at Sátoraljaújhely, was deported to the Auschwitz concentration camp on May 20, 1944. Her trail follows closely that of her sister Laura. Their names appear one right after the other on every transport list, their prisoner numbers only one digit apart, just as my mother had always told me. It seems that the prisoner number was the most important identification method for the inmates of concentration camps; their names were secondary.

Even Laura and Sidonia's Dachau questionnaires are similar, except for some of the features in their physical description and Sidonia's prisoner number, 86794. My mother's height measured 170 centimeters, or five feet seven inches (a couple inches taller than her actual height), *Face: oval, Eyes: brown, Teeth: healthy.* Here is proof again of one of my mother's false birth dates, as the document shows her birth year as 1915, two years younger than her actual date of birth.

After my mother's liberation from the Bergen Belsen concentration camp, many documents show her name as a survivor. It is listed in various publications, including *Sharit Haplatah* (Counted Remnant), the book containing the list of survivors in displaced persons camps. In the spring of 2011, I received the most recent documents, showing my mother and me on the list of emigrants from Germany to the United States of America. These include "The International Refugee Organization, Master List No. 2, 'Youth Argosy,' 'Basis for Future Flights,' Wentorf near Hamburg, Germany" and "International Refugee Organization, DP Emigration to

United States of America, Sailing Ex Bremerhaven for New York, N.Y., June 23, 1949, on USAT 'General Howze.'"

(Kis) Etu Deutsch, my mother's friend and step-niece, also known as Eta, Etel, and Etelka, was arrested in May 1944 and fell under the control of the Hungarian police. She was then arrested in Riga on August 9, 1944, and transferred to the Stutthof concentration camp on August 16, 1944. On September 30, 1944, she was transferred to the Buchenwald concentration camp, assigned to forced labor, and later transferred from the main camp at Buchenwald to the work camp at ATG–Leipzig. On February 19, 1945, she was transferred from Leipzig to Bernberg. She appears on the list "Hungarian Women Formerly at Leipzig Found in Wurzen," dated June 30,1945, after the close of the war. She returned to Hungary after the war, married again, bore two children, and departed from Hungary with her family in 1956, arriving in New York by way of Austria in 1959. In 2009, once I had the information about Etu in my possession, I contacted her two children. They advised me of their mother's death in New York in 2005, only a year before my mother's death. Neither of the friends, Etu or my mother, ever knew each other's location.

All the information from ITS arrived by e-mail. Thus, when I logged on to my computer to read my e-mails one day, it was with immense shock and trepidation that I found five messages from the United States Holocaust Memorial Museum with a subject line that read "Perlstein, Dezso." I knew before opening them that I would discover much more about my uncle's wartime experiences than I could ever have imagined. I was not sure I wanted to know about them.

My mother was always calmed by the thought that her brother had died in Auschwitz. Perhaps he had been spared the cruelty that she and Laura had confronted when they were transferred to other camps. Not knowing his fate was somehow reassuring, for both of us. Yet, the implication of seeing those five messages was that our consoling thoughts had just been dreams. After his deportation, Dezso had lived long enough to have the events in his life fill five e-mail messages and attachments. I made myself wait at least another day to open them. This was what I found:

Dezso Perlstein fell subject to detention at Vencsello, Szabolcs county, Hungary, on April 17, 1944. From there, he was deported to Auschwitz on May 27, 1944, but remained there only ten days. He was transferred to the Buchenwald concentration camp on June 6, 1944. Soon later, on June 15, 1944, he was transferred again to the "Willie" subcamp, but he was returned a few days later to the main camp along with a number of other prisoners. On June 20, 1944, he was transferred within the camp from block 17 to block 55.

Dezso's Buchenwald prisoner questionnaire, administered using the same form as in Dachau, completed in ink, includes the following (translated) biographical and descriptive information:

> *Perlstein Dezso, born on October 16, 1900, in Dámóc,*
> > *Prisoner Number 57569*
> *Place of residence: Vencsello, Desseffy 67, Szabolcs county*
> *Occupation: Worker [Arbeiter]*
> *Status: Married*
> *Name of spouse: Serina, born Schönberger*
> *Place of residence: Concentration Camp Auschwitz*
> *Children: three, 6–10 years old*
> *Education: sixth grade*
> *Wartime service: Infantry, 1918*
> *Height: 174 [centimeters, or five feet, eight and one half inch-*
> > *es], Shape: slender, Face: long, Eyes: gray, Nose: curved,*
> > *Mouth: large, Ears: large, Teeth: 8 missing, Hair: dark*
> > *brown, Language: Hungarian, German*

On October 26, 1944, Dezso is listed on a Buchenwald medical report that notes the names and numbers of prisoners seen by physicians whose purpose was to determine each prisoner's suitability for work or transport. Dezso is listed under the heading "Those only suitable for light work." Another medical report on November 28, 1944, then finds him "capable of either work or transport." On December 13, he was transported again, this time to the subcamp of Berga, where he died on February 22, 1945. An ITS–created death certificate indicates the cause of his death as *Akute Herzschwäche*, acute heart failure.

Dezso Perlstein's death certificate. Cause of death (akute Herzschwäche): acute heart failure. Courtesy of the United States Holocaust Memorial Museum and the International Tracing Service.

More than sixty years after his death, I mourned for my Uncle Dezso as though it had happened the day I discovered it in an e-mail. It did not matter that his demise had occurred a long time ago. Once he was an adventurer, a rascal who sometimes tried to outsmart the authorities in making illegal border crossings and daring escapades. As his Buchenwald questionnaire indicates, he was a married man with three children all under the age of ten whose wife was also a concentration camp prisoner at Auschwitz. An infantryman during World War 1, when he was only eighteen years old, he had fought for his country, Hungary, on the losing side of that horrible conflict. Yet, he had risked his life for his homeland. Later, the same homeland for which he fought abandoned him, allowing him to endure the torture of deportation and forced labor and, eventually, death at the age of forty-four, alone, no one knowing of his agony.

Now I am the one who knows, the only one left to mourn for him and for his siblings, parents, wife, and children, all but Sidonia gone from the face of the earth as though they had never existed. I will never know the exact date of death of most of my ancestors, but I have added one more loved one to my small list of those for whom I can say the Kaddish prayers, and remember them on their Yahrzeit:

Hani Klein Perlstein died on the eighth day of the Hebrew month of Nissan.
Sidonia Perlstein died on the sixteenth day of Iyar.
Dezso Perlstein died on the ninth day of Adar.

Hanna Marcus

Sidonia's Thread

Hanna Perlstein Marcus

090641